VEGETARIAN NOSH FOR STUDENTS

by Joy May & the family team

THE NOSH SERIES OF COOKBOOKS BY JOY MAY

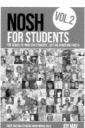

ISBN: 9780956746474

ISBN: 9780956746467

ISBN: 9780954317973

ISBN: 9780956746481

ISBN: 9780956746443

ISBN: 9780956746450

ISBN: 9780956746498

ISBN: 9780993260919

NEW

 @NOSHBOOKS

WE WOULD LOVE HEAR FROM YOU. USE
#NOSHBOOKS

contents

Introduction

I am excited about getting young people to cook good, healthy meals from non-processed food sources. This edition of Vegetarian Nosh for Students is packed with yummy recipes and ideas for vegetarian students.

Having had two sons go through Uni, I know the restrictions and hazards of student kitchens. With this in mind, I have made the book as straightforward as possible. At the same time, I have introduced a good variety of ingredients to give vegetarians a healthy balanced diet and possibly to introduce them to some new foodstuffs.

Cooking vegetarian food requires a little more thinking out of the box, or you will end up eating the same cheese on toast or stir-fry all the time. This book aims to inspire to greater heights.

The layout makes cooking easy and inspiring: there is a photo of each recipe that should help. There are also some weekly menu and shopping plans.

The recipes are planned so that you need to use the minimum of pans, dishes and utensils. You need use no weighing scales. There is also a list of stuff you need to take to Uni to help you cook.

Simple Key

How much it will cost per person.

£0.80 /PERSON

How easy it is to make. 1 star being super-easy and 5 stars more adventurous.

3

How many people the recipe will feed.

2

How long it will take to prepare the meal.

PREP 15 MINS

How long it takes to cook the food (oven or hob).

COOK 20 MINS

How long you might have to leave the food to cool in the fridge or freezer.

COOL 2 HRS

Recipe costs

The recipe costs in this book are an average between Tesco and Sainsbury's and are the prices at the time of writing. To keep the pricing very relevant, we will update each new print run. Last update **April 2016**.

One of the key features of this book is that you do not need weighing scales and special measuring equipment. These things are scarcely found in student accommodation.

Throughout the book I have used a mug to measure ingredients. This mug holds $1/2$ a pint of liquid and is the size of the mug pictured opposite.

a mug =

ACTUAL SIZE

All you need

The following is all you will need to be able to cook every recipe in this book:

- [x] mug (approx. 1/2 pint)
- [x] tablespoon, one mum serves with
- [x] dessertspoon, one you eat cereal with
- [x] teaspoon, one you stir tea with
- [x] wooden spoon
- [x] chopping board
- [x] sharp knife
- [x] small pan with lid
- [x] medium-sized pan, with lid
- [x] slotted turner (fish slice)
- [x] frying pan
- [x] wok is useful, but not essential
- [x] casserole dish, with lid
- [x] colander
- [x] flat roasting dish, or metal non-stick cooking tray
- [x] cheese grater
- [x] hand-held blender
- [x] sieve
- [x] loaf tin
- [x] mixing bowl

Good buying ideas

It is good to **plan a menu for the week.** This makes cooking much easier, since you will not be dashing to the shops the whole time for little things. It also means you will not waste food, as you will just buy what you need for the week. Try the planner on the opposite page.

Look at page 12. **Make sure that you are getting a balanced diet.** Decide before you go to the shops what kind of vegetables and fruits you need to buy. Fruit and veg are best eaten when fresh, because the minerals and vitamins deteriorate after 2–3 days.

Always make sure that when you have visited home, you return to uni having **creamed off any 'excess'** from mum's cupboards.

You will need to **build up a stock of herbs and spices** in order to keep your food tasty and varied. Buy in bulk from Asian supermarkets they cost a fraction of the price. Keep them in sealed packets or jars and they will maintain their flavour for a long time.

Nuts and dried fruits are sometimes cheaper in places like **Holland and Barrett and Julian Graves.**

If you are sharing accommodation with other vegetarians, **share the cooking with them**. You cook one day and they the next. This will not only save you time and hassle, but cooking in larger quantities will save you money in the long run.

weekly Food planner

This menu should cost approximately **£18 for the week.**

This plan assumes that you will eat sandwiches and fruit for lunch each day and cereal or toast for breakfast.

Shopping List

- cereal for breakfast
- milk
- bread for sandwiches
- sandwich fillings
- 2 medium sweet potatoes
- 1 large potato
- 3 onions
- 2 mushrooms
- 1 carrot
- 1 head of celery
- 1 red pepper
- 1 small lettuce
- 1 tomato
- 1 tin tomatoes
- 1 small tin sweetcorn
- 1 packet spaghetti
- Parmesan-style cheese
- 250g Cheddar cheese
- 1 small carton fromage frais
- 1 small carton natural yogurt
- 200g pack cashew nuts
- 1 leek
- fresh ginger
- 1 lemon
- 2 spring onions
- 1 small cucumber

Menu

Monday	Spag Bol p108
Tuesday	Rest of Spag Bol
Wednesday	Baked Potato and Cheese p24
Thursday	Sweet Potato Patties p93
Friday	Rest of Sweet Potato
Saturday	½ quantity of French Onion Soup p55
Sunday	Classic Nut Roast—share with a friend p156

check cupboards for:

- oil
- stock cubes
- oregano
- Marmite
- sugar
- red lentils
- garlic
- honey
- mixed herbs

For more weekly food plans see pages 200-203

Storecupboard and Fridge

Here are some basics to keep in your storecupboard and fridge. Usually in student halls, or shared houses, you will have a shelf in the fridge, one drawer in the freezer and a cupboard to yourself.

FRIDGE/FREEZER

- spare loaf of bread in freezer
- spare pint of milk in freezer (plastic not glass bottles)
- butter/spread
- milk
- eggs
- cheese
- mayo
- curry paste
- Quorn

STORECUPBOARD

- rice
- pasta
- cereal
- tin of chopped tomatoes
- tin of baked beans
- tins of beans and pulses
- dried lentils and pulses
- tofu
- pilau rice seasoning (livens up rice)
- soy sauce
- curry paste (put in fridge once open)
- oil to cook with
- salt and pepper
- vegetable stock cubes
- cornflour
- tomato purée
- Marmite
- sugar
- flour
- cornflour
- useful herbs and spices
- mixed dried herbs
- dried basil
- chilli flakes
- paprika

Good things to eat

You will know, as a vegetarian, that it is important for you to think carefully about the food you eat. Eating loads of pasta, cheese and vegetables, is not really sufficient. There are many good sources of proteins, vitamins, and minerals to be found. Below are some general guidelines to eating healthily as a vegetarian.

RECOMMENDED DAILY INTAKE:
(NOTE, ONE PORTION = ONE SERVING OR 1 PIECE FRUIT)

3–4	portions of cereals, grains, or potatoes
4–5	portions of fruit, or vegetables (1 glass of real fruit juice counts as 1 portion)
2–3	portions of pulses, nuts, or seeds
2	portions of milk, cheese, eggs, or soya
A small quantity	vegetable oil, butter, or margarine

Carbohydrates. These are our main energy source. However, too much carbohydrate is not good for you. Sources include bread, white rice, potatoes and other root vegetables, pasta, flour, cereal, sweets and chocolate.

Proteins. These are 'body builders', not just to develop muscle, but to keep our cartilage, hair, skin and blood in good shape. Sources include dairy products, grains, cereals, pulses, seeds, nuts, Quorn, tofu and eggs.

Fats. We do need some fat in our diet, but it is essential not to overdo it. Eat fats which are high in monounsaturated and polyunsaturated fats.

Vitamins and Minerals. If you eat a balanced diet, you will get the vitamins and minerals you need. Milk is an excellent balanced food. Milk is rich in minerals, vitamins and calcium and is also high in protein, carbohydrate and fat. Skimmed or semi-skimmed is the best. You need to make sure you get enough iron, in order to keep your blood count healthy. Iron is found in some unrefined cereals, pulses, beans and lentils. Fruit, vegetables and nuts provide a wide range of vitamins and minerals.

Soya and microproteins. Soya is a vegetable protein and contains amino acids (good for you). Soya beans are low in cholesterol and unsaturated fats and high in calcium. Sources: soya milk, soya sauce, textured vegetable protein (TVP) and tofu. Tofu contains calcium, iron and vitamins B1, B2, and B3.

Fruit and Vegetables. Provide fibre, essential in our diet, together with vitamins and minerals. Root vegetables, potatoes, carrots, swedes, etc. are not good in excess, as they are high in carbohydrates. Fresh and dried fruit and fruit smoothies make excellent, high nutrition, snacks.

Spirulina is known as a modern 'superfood'. It is known to significantly increase energy and stamina levels, as well as boost the immune system. It is an excellent food supplement for vegetarians. Buy from the Internet or Holland and Barrett.

If, on any one day, you choose to make a dish that has only vegetables, make sure that you eat some soya, nuts and/or cheese. Have fresh and dried fruit and nuts to hand and get into the habit of eating them. If, by the end of the week, you have fruit that needs eating, make a smoothie!

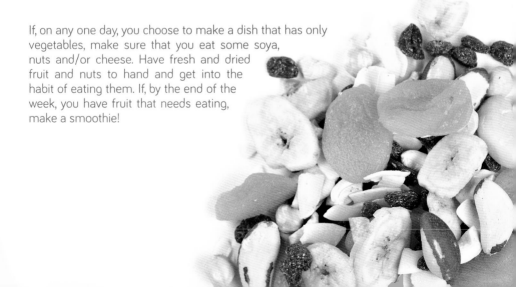

Things to look out for

If you are new to being vegetarian, it is easy to accidentally eat things that contain traces of meat product. Listed opposite are some potential pitfalls relevant to the recipes in this book.

See www.vegsoc.org for an extended list.

Health food shops are good places to source vegetarian foods. The staff know what they are talking about. Nuts and dried fruits are usually much cheaper there than in the supermarkets.

When shopping, read the labels carefully. You will soon find good sources of vegetarian foods. Look for Vegetarian Society approved products.

POTENTIAL PITFALLS

Additives/ E numbers	certain additives in foods may not be vegetarian, for example, cochineal sometimes present in glacé cherries. Buy cochineal-free cherries.
Bread	some bakers may grease the tins with animal fat, check your local baker.
Butter	make sure you buy pure butter.
Cheese	may have been produced using animal rennet. Look for vegetarian alternatives.
Chocolate	can contain whey and emulsifiers, check the labels.
Crisps	the flavourings may contain whey, some crisps may be made with yeast extract.
Curry paste	Thai curry paste may contain fish or fish sauce. Indian curry pastes are usually OK.
Egg noodles	make sure they are made from free-range eggs, or look for eggless noodles, e.g. rice noodles.
Eggs	we recommend that you only use free-range eggs.
Gelatine	made from animal source, sometimes in sweets and desserts.
GM foods	are to be avoided.
Margarines	may contain animal fats or fish oils. Buy olive oil spreads.
Mayonnaise	may contain eggs which are not free-range. Check labels or look for vegetarian variety.
Parmesan cheese	is usually not vegetarian, look for a Parmesan-style vegetarian cheese.
Pasta	may not be made with free-range eggs, check the label.
Stock	buy vegetarian and make sure does not contain animal fats.
Tofu	can sometimes be GM.
Wine vinegars, alcohol & juices	may be refined with a non vegetarian source, read labels carefully.
Yogurts, cream & crème fraîche	some of these may contain gelatine.
Flour	may contain 'flour improvers', which could come from animal sources

How long can I keep this before it kills me?

HOW LONG CAN I KEEP THINGS?

Eggs	1 month from lay date (usually the use-by date on the egg).
Milk	2-3 days once opened. If unopened see 'best-before' date.
Butter and margarine	6 weeks
Cheese	1 week once opened, 2 weeks unopened. Keep cheese wrapped.
Onions and potatoes	1 week, best out of the fridge and in a dark place.
Green vegetables	1 week in fridge.
Carrots, parsnips, etc.	1 week in fridge.
Salad, lettuce, cucumber, tomatoes, peppers, etc.	1 week in fridge.
Leftovers	ONLY the day after the food has been cooked. All kinds of nasties can begin to lurk there.

Sell-by dates are when the store needs to sell things by. **Use-by dates** are indications that you should not be eating them after said date.

Here are some basic guidelines that should help you avoid making yourself ill:

HOW DO I KNOW IF SOMETHING IS PAST IT?

Cheese	Green mould on the surface.
Potatoes	Skin is turning green and excessive 'ears'.
Yogurts	Lid 'puffing up'. If opened, the smell changes and it tastes 'sharp'.
Bread	Mould around the crust.
Vegetables	Originally crisp vegetables now soft and soggy, e.g. 'bendy' carrots.

Reheating food

Take care when reheating food, that you **heat it thoroughly.** It should be 'piping hot'. This means all the food should be steaming and the plate needs a cloth to get it out of the microwave.

To reheat a plate of food in the microwave, **cover it with cling film and place on a high heat,** for approximately 3½ mins in a 600watt microwave. However, refer to the point above if you are unsure.

Storing stuff

A few plastic, sealable boxes and some cling film are essentials when sharing a fridge while you are in halls or house sharing. If you share with those who eat meat or keep unacceptable stuff in the fridge, keep things wrapped and your food should stay OK.

If you cook a meal one day, **eat any leftovers the next day** and not after that.

Be very careful with rice, cool it quickly and place it in the fridge.

Don't keep opened tins in the fridge; a chemical reaction occurs, affecting the food, once the tin is open to the air. Transfer any excess to a bowl and cover with cling film.

Keep potatoes out of the fridge in a cool dark place, can be inside a cupboard. This stops them going green so quickly.

Nuts and dried fruits—invest in a packet of clothes pegs and seal any opened packets with them. If you have the room, keep them all in a large plastic box.

Seven steps to success

Here are some things that will help you enjoy cooking and hopefully minimise discouraging failures.

1 Plan what you will eat, and **shop for the week** all in one go. This saves time and money as you will not buy stuff you don't need. At the back of the book you will find sample menus for a week. Once you are used to using these, you can make your own menus and shopping lists.

2 **Try to keep things varied**, e.g. don't cook the same stir-fry over and over again. Try new recipes, gradually stock up on the more unusual ingredients.

3 When frying vegetables, especially onions, **make sure you take the time to allow them to brown.** This caramelises the starches and sugars in the food, and gives them a much better taste.

4 **Try to keep things clean in the kitchen**, e.g. chopping boards, dish cloths and tea towels. Even though you are not dealing with meat yourself, if others in the kitchen are, then you need to take extra care.

5 **Prepare all the ingredients** before you begin to cook. For example: don't try to chop vegetables whilst you are frying other things.

6 **Read the recipe** all the way through, before you begin, in order to get a clear idea of what you are doing.

7 **Start by cooking the easy things** you know and like, if you are not a confident cook.

What do I do if...

...everything I cook in the oven is burnt or undercooked?

It could be, that if you have an older oven, the thermostat is not working quite as well as it should. Don't give up, just adjust by raising or lowering the temperature you set it to. Also, the temperatures in some ovens can vary a great deal, depending on which shelf you put your food on. Where possible use middle shelves. Check what kind of oven you have: Centigrade, Centigrade fan oven or Fahrenheit oven. Then check the temperature on the recipe.

...I don't have a microwave to defrost food?

Keep the food in the freezer bag and place in cold water, don't use boiling water. The best thing is to plan ahead, take food out of the freezer and leave in the fridge overnight to defrost.

...I don't have a lid for my casserole dish?

Cover it with foil and scrunch the edges to seal to the dish.

...sauces go lumpy?

Put them in a jug or bowl and whizz them with a hand-held blender.

...everything I cook on top of the cooker is burnt?

Either you need to keep the heat turned down, or just keep an eye on things. You can't go off and ring your mates, whilst trying to cook.

...I have made things too spicy?

With chilli dishes, just try adding another tin of tomatoes. With a curry, peel and cut a potato into four and add to the curry, simmer for 10 minutes and remove potato.

...everything seems tasteless?

Remember to season well as you cook.

Veggies
Boiling

Generally, most vegetables need to be cooked in just enough water to cover them.

1. Bring the water to the boil.
2. Once boiling, add the vegetables and a little salt and simmer gently, with the lid on the pan. If you keep the source of the heat low, you will preserve a little more of the nutrition in the vegetables.

BOILING TIMES

Swedes and turnips	2–3cm chunks	20–25 mins
Potatoes	2–3cm chunks	10–15 mins
Parsnips, carrots	cut into 2cm rings	10–15 mins
Cauliflower	broken into little trees	10 mins
Broccoli	broken into little trees	5 mins
Green beans	cut off the stalk and tail	5 mins
Spinach	take off any thick stalks	30 secs–1 min
Leeks	cut into 2cm rings	5 mins
Cabbage	cut into long thin strips	5 mins
Sugar snaps	leave as they are	2 mins
Mangetout	leave as they are	1 min

Note
For **spinach**, cook just enough to make the leaves wilt. You will only need a quarter of a mug of water in the bottom of the pan.

For **cabbage**, use half a mug of water in the pan, drain after cooking and add some butter and black pepper. Return to the pan and cook for another 2 minutes, to dry the cabbage a little.

Roasting

1. Preheat the oven to 180°C fan oven/200°C/Gas 6.

2. Put the vegetables on a flat roasting/baking tray and sprinkle them with salt and olive oil. Turn them over with your hands, to make sure that the oil is covering all the pieces. Set them on the tray with flat sides up. If the flat sides are on the tray itself they will tend to stick. Sprinkle with rosemary if you wish.

3. Put in the middle of the oven for 30 minutes. Check to see if any are getting too brown, maybe the ones around the edge. Move, or turn over as necessary. Put back in the oven for another 20 minutes. You can put a mix of veg in (see photo below). If you are roasting individual veg, see timings below:

ROASTING TIMES

Potatoes	cut into 5–6cm chunks	40–50 mins
Butternut squash	peel, cut into 5–6cm chunks	30–40 mins
Parsnips	cut into 4, lengthways	40–45 mins
Sweet potatoes	peel, cut into 5–6cm chunks	40–50 mins
Onions	cut into 6 wedges	40–50 mins
Fennel	cut into 4 wedges	30–40 mins
Tomatoes	cut the skin	20–25 mins
Peppers	remove seeds and stalk, cut into large pieces	25 mins

Joy has done a great video on how to make those fluffy roast potatoes your mum makes for Sunday roasts noshbooks.com/fluffy

Perfect rice every time

There are many different types of rice to buy. I would recommend that you use basmati. It is slightly more expensive than long grain or quick-cook rice, but has a much better flavour and texture than the cheaper varieties.

$$\text{rice for 1 person} = \tfrac{1}{2} \text{ mug rice} + 1 \text{ mug water}$$

(+ 1 teaspoon of pilau rice seasoning, optional, but gives a yummy flavour.)

1. Using a pan with a lid, bring the water to the boil, add the seasoning and stir until it has dissolved.

2. Add the rice and stir once, bring back to the boil. Once boiling, turn down the heat to very low, so that the rice simmers gently. Put the lid on the pan and cook for approximately 15 minutes. Do not stir whilst the rice is cooking, or you will make it sticky. The rice should be cooked once the water has disappeared. Check occasionally to see if the water has boiled away.

3. Test the rice once the water has boiled away. If the rice is still too crunchy and the water has all gone, then you have boiled it too quickly. Add a little more water, replace the lid and cook for another 5 minutes.

Joy did a video of this, check it out at noshbooks.com/rice

How to cook pasta

There are innumerable kinds of pasta to choose from in the shops, made from different ingredients. Most will have instructions on the packets as to how to cook them. Just in case you have lost the packet, here are some general guidelines:

Spaghetti

1. Use the guide above to measure the quantities required for 1–4 people. Boil sufficient water in a pan to cover the spaghetti whilst cooking.

2. Once the water is boiling, lower the spaghetti sticks into the water. Once the half that is in the water has softened slightly, push the other half in. Simmer for 6–8 minutes.

3. Test one piece to see if it is cooked. Drain the water off and add one teaspoon of butter or olive oil. Mix around and this will stop the spaghetti sticking together.

Most other pastas

Again, boil enough water to cover the pasta. Once the water is boiling, add the pasta. **One mug of dried pasta is plenty for one person with a very healthy appetite.** Simmer for the appropriate time, drain and add butter or olive oil to prevent the pasta sticking together.

Here is a guide, but it still depends on the thickness of the pasta:
Tagliatelle - the stuff that comes in little nests. 4–5 minutes.
Spaghetti - 6 minutes, depending how thick the spaghetti is.
Radiatore - looks like little radiators. 10 minutes.
Fusilli - little twists. 6–8 minutes.
Penne - little tubes, vary in size. 10–12 minutes.
Conchiglie - little shells. 6–8 minutes.
Macaroni - 12–15 minutes.
Farfalle - looks like little bows. 6–8 minutes.

Use medium **Jacket potato** or large potatoes. Always make a cut in the skin with a knife before baking, or it may explode in the oven or the microwave. You will only get the crisp jackets if you cook the potato in the oven. Timing depends on the size of the potato.

Oven baked — Preheat the oven to 200°C fan oven/220°C/Gas 7, bake for 50–60 minutes.
Microwave and oven — Preheat the oven to 200°C fan oven/220°C/Gas 7. Cook in the microwave on full power for 5 minutes and then in the oven for 30 minutes.
Microwave — 7–10 minutes on full power.

Fillings

When the potato is cooked, cut it open and add a little butter to moisten, then add any of the following suggestions:

1 **The simplest**—Baked beans and/or grated cheese.

2 **Cheesy chives**—Mix together 1/2 x 125g packet of soft cream cheese, 2 dessertspoons fromage frais, 2 x 2cm cubes of blue cheese, crumbled, 1 stick of finely chopped celery, 1 teaspoon chives and 2 chopped spring onions. Season with salt and pepper. (You can vary this recipe using different kinds of cheese, strong ones are best.)

3 **Potato baked twice, with pesto**—Cut the baked potato in half, lengthways. Scoop out the soft potato with a spoon, being careful not to break the skin. Place in a dish and mash with a fork. Mix in 1 tablespoon of thick double cream, 1 teaspoon of vegetarian green pesto sauce, a squeeze of lemon juice and one teaspoon of pine nuts. Season with salt and pepper. Put the potato mixture back into the skin and grate some Parmesan-style cheese over the top. Return to the oven for 20 minutes until the cheese has browned.

4 **Egg and Mayo and sweetcorn**—Hard boil 2 eggs (see page 30). Peel off the shell and roughly chop. Add 1 tablespoon of mayonnaise, half a small tin of sweetcorn and season well with salt and pepper.

5 **Cheese and Mushroom**—Finely chop a small garlic clove and fry in a little butter for 30 seconds. Add 3 sliced mushrooms and 1/2 teaspoon of dried mixed herbs. Cook for 1 minute. Take off the heat and add a good tablespoon of cream cheese. Season well.

6 **Roasted veg**—Peel a sweet potato, cut into 2 cm chunks, 1/2 red pepper, cut into 8 pieces, 1 finely chopped garlic glove, 1/2 an onion, chopped, 1 tomato, cut into 4, and 3 - 4 black olives. Place on a baking tray and drizzle over with oil. Season well, mix together and place in the oven 30 minutes before the potato is cooked.

sandwiches **interesting** sandwiches
sandwiches sandwiches
sandwiches sandwiches
sandwiches sandwiches
sandwiches sandwiches
sandwiches sandwiches
sandwiches sandwiches
sandwiches sandwiches
sandwiches sandwiches
sandwiches sandwiches
sandwiches sandwiches

It is important to eat good bread, look out for granary and wholemeal. Try not to eat white bread all the time. Pitta bread will hold a bit more filling; iceberg lettuce works well as a filling, because it gives a crispy contrast to the pitta.

Poached egg and wilted spinach

Heat a small amount of oil in a frying pan, add the spinach and cook for 30 seconds, the spinach will wilt. Set to one side while you poach an egg (see page 30). Put together in the sandwich and season well.

Scrambled eggs and cheese and tomato

Grate 1/2 mug cheese. Chop a tomato quite finely. Heat a little butter in a small non-stick saucepan, add the tomatoes and fry for 1 minute. Add 2 eggs and cook until they begin to set. Add the cheese and cook for 30 seconds. Season well and make the sandwich while the eggs are still hot.

Egg mayo

Hard boil 2 eggs (see page 30). Rinse them under cold water, take off the shells and chop them up with a knife. Mix them together with 1 tablespoon mayo and season with salt and pepper.

Cream cheese and banana

Spread one slice of the bread with a good helping of cream cheese. Slice a banana and place on top. Spread the other slice of bread with honey or jam and press together lightly.

Feta cheese

Crumble the cheese and add iceberg lettuce, sliced tomatoes, some chopped-up spring onions and a dessertspoon of mayo.

Roasted aubergine with homemade houmous

Buy a small aubergine and cut into three, lengthways. Sprinkle with a little oil and season well. Place in a hot oven (200C fan oven/220C/Gas 7) for 25 minutes. Meanwhile make some houmous. Put a 400g tin of chickpeas in a bowl, together with 1 tablespoon oil, juice of one lemon, 1 teaspoon tahini paste (optional) and season well. Whizz with the hand-held blender. Once the aubergine is cooked, place in the sandwich with some of the houmous and eat while still warm.

Salad with fried halloumi

Cut the halloumi into 1cm slices and fry in a little oil, on a high heat, until brown. This will just take a minute or so. Put some lettuce, tomato and a finely chopped spring onion in the sandwich and add the fried cheese.

Stuff on toast

Cheese on toast
with a little something extra.

1. Very lightly toast the bread under a hot grill, since you will return it to the grill later to cook the cheese.

2. Butter the toast. At this stage you can add things to go under the cheese, such as pickle, Marmite, or sliced tomatoes.

3. Slice or grate the cheese and place on top. Make sure the cheese covers the edges of the toast; it will protect the corners of the bread from being burned. Use a slotted turner to put the toast back under the grill.

4. Cook until the cheese begins to bubble.

Eggie bread

1. Break an egg into a mug and beat with a fork. Pour out onto a plate.

2. Dip one side of a thick slice of bread into the egg, quickly turn over and let the other side soak up the rest of the egg.

3. Put a 2cm cube of butter in a frying pan and heat gently until the butter starts to bubble.

4. Add the bread and cook, turning over to brown both sides.

5. Serve with beans, HP or tomato sauce. To make it into breakfast serve with honey, or maple syrup and sliced fruit.

Beans on toast with egg on top
Toast the bread, heat the beans, and then fry or poach the eggs (page 30). Great with HP sauce.

Welsh Rarebit
1/2 mug grated **Cheddar cheese**
2 teaspoons **flour**
1/2 mug **milk**
1/2 teaspoon **mustard**
1/2 teaspoon **HP Sauce**
1 **egg yolk**
2cm cube **butter**

1. Without the heat on, put the grated cheese and the flour in a small saucepan and mix well.

2. Add the rest of the ingredients and mix well.

3. Heat slowly until the mixture thickens and is hot. Serve on a thick slice of toast.

Garlic bread
This works best with medium-sized bread sticks.

1. Finely chop 1 garlic clove, and mix together with about 3cm cube of butter. You could add 1 teaspoon of dried chives at this point if you wish.

2. Make diagonal cuts in the bread stick, but not quite all the way through.

3. Push the garlic butter into the cuts in the bread. Don't use loads, because it will be very greasy if you do.

4. Wrap the bread stick in foil and bake in the oven for 7–8 minutes (200°C fan oven/220°C/Gas 7).

Eggs

Boil

1. Using a small pan, fill 2/3 full with water and bring to the boil.
2. Lower the egg into the pan on a spoon.
3. Simmer briskly for 3 minutes for a very runny egg, 5 minutes and you will still be able to dip your soldiers in the runny yolk, 12 minutes and it will be hard-boiled.

Poach

1. Using a small pan, or frying pan, half fill with water and add a good pinch of salt. Bring to the boil, then turn down, until the water is only just moving.
2. Break the egg into a mug or cup, gently pour into the water. Do not stir or turn the heat up, just let it cook gently. It will take 2–4 minutes, depending on the size of the egg.
3. Once the egg has gone opaque, gently lift out with a slotted turner and let the water drain from it.

Fry

1. Heat 2 teaspoons butter in the frying pan, until the butter just bubbles.
2. Break the egg into a mug and then gently pour into the frying pan.
3. Cook on medium/low heat, until the egg is set.
4. Using a slotted turner, turn the egg over half-way through cooking if you want 'easy over' hard yolk.

Scramble

1. Using a small milk pan, preferably non-stick, add 2 teaspoons butter, heat gently until the butter bubbles.
2. Break the egg into the pan and add salt and pepper. Stir slowly, breaking up the egg yolk.
3. When the egg is almost set, take off the heat. The egg will continue to cook in its own heat. If you cook it too long it will become rubbery.
4. You can add grated cheese and/or chopped tomatoes half-way through the cooking.

Omelettes

Instructions for a basic omelette for 1 person

1. Put two or three eggs in a mug and beat well with a fork, add two tablespoons of water.

2. Switch on the grill to full heat, to warm up.

3. Melt about a dessertspoon of butter in the frying pan. Once it begins to 'bubble' pour the egg mixture into the pan.

4. As the egg begins to set on the bottom of the pan, gently move the set egg with fish slice and allow the runny egg to take its place. Do this with two or three sweeping movements, don't stir, or you will get scrambled egg. If you are making double quantity, repeat this process once more.

5. While there is still a little runny egg on the top, take off the heat, add whatever filling you want, top with cheese (not essential) and place the frying pan under the hot grill. The omelette should rise. Once it is browned on the top, remove from the grill and turn out onto a plate. Serve with salad, garlic bread or baked potatoes.

Suggested fillings – cheese, tomato, mushrooms, fried onions, chopped spring onions, wilted spinach (page 20), or any combination of these ingredients.

Joy has done a simple video on how to cook an omelette. Check it out at noshbooks.com/soup

Sauces

Some vegetarian dishes tend to be a little dry. **Here are a few different sauces that you can use to enhance meals.** Try them out and see which ones you like. All will keep in the fridge for a couple of days.

Sweet and Sour Sauce

2 tablespoons **tomato purée**

3 tablespoons **sugar**

2 tablespoons **white wine vinegar**

1 tablespoon **soy sauce**

2 teaspoons **cornflour**

1 mug **water**

1. Mix the cornflour and the water in a saucepan until smooth.

2. Add the rest of the ingredients and bring to the boil. The sauce should thicken.

Piquant Tomato Sauce

1 tablespoon of **oil** to fry

1 **onion**, sliced

400g **tin tomatoes**

1 teaspoon **black pepper**

1 tablespoon **tomato purée**

1 tablespoon **white wine vinegar**

1 teaspoon **sugar**

1. Heat the oil in a saucepan, add the tomatoes and fry until the onions come soft.

2. Add the rest of the ingredients and bring to the boil simmer for 2–3 minutes.

3. Blitz with a hand-held blender if you have one, or use as it is.

Pepper Sauce

1¹/₂ red **peppers**, chopped

¹/₂ **onion**, sliced

1 **clove garlic**, chopped

1 tablespoon **cream**

¹/₂ teaspoon **sugar**

salt and **pepper**

1. Fry the peppers, onions, and garlic in a saucepan, over a medium heat, for 5–8 minutes, until they are really soft.

2. Add the sugar and cream and mix.

3. Use the hand-held blender to liquidise, or leave as it is.

4. Add the cream, and season well with salt and freshly ground black pepper. You can add half a teaspoon of chilli powder if you like.

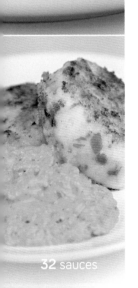

Quick Cheese Sauce

1 mug grated **cheese**
1 tablespoon **flour**
1cm cube **butter**

1 mug **milk**
1/8 teaspoon **paprika**
salt and **pepper**

1. Without the heat on, put the grated cheese into a saucepan, add the flour, salt, pepper and paprika and stir well.

2. Add the milk and butter. Put on a low heat and bring to the boil, stirring all the time, the sauce should thicken.

Use this sauce as a pasta sauce, for veggie bakes, lasagna and cauliflower cheese.

Tomato Sauce

1 **onion**, chopped
1 clove **garlic**, finely chopped
1 tin **chopped tomatoes**
2 teaspoons **tomato purée**
1 teaspoon **sugar**
salt and **pepper**

1 teaspoon **herbs**
1 **vegetable stock cube**, crumbled
1/4 mug **water**
1 tablespoon **oil** to fry

1. Fry the onions and garlic in oil, for 4–5 minutes.
2. Add the rest of the ingredients and bring to the boil.
3. Turn down to simmer for 10 minutes.
4. Whizz with a blender. You can add HP sauce or chilli sauce if you wish.

Peanut Sauce

2 tablespoons crunchy **peanut butter**
1 dessertspoon **soy sauce**
2 tablespoons **coconut milk**

1 teaspoon **tomato purée**
1 teaspoon **sugar**

1. Mix everything together and you are ready to go!

Smoothies

Healthy and tasty, try some of these smoothies. You will need a hand-held blender and a jug to blend the fruits in. Once you have had a go at these ones, experiment with your own variations

Serves: 1-2 people   Preparation time: 2 mins

Melon, strawberries and yogurt

¼ of a **melon**
6-7 **strawberries**
1 tablespoon **yogurt**.

Cut up all the fruit and add to the yogurt and whizz in a jug.

Oranges

grated rind and flesh of an **orange**
1 **eating apple**, peeled and chopped **apple juice**

Whizz together and add enough juice to make a drinking consistency.

Strawberries

a handful of **strawberries**
1 tablespoon of **strawberry yogurt**
a few drops of **vanilla extract**
a little **apple juice**, or **milk**.

Whizz together and add enough juice, or milk, to make a drinking consistency.

Banana, honey and yogurt

1 **banana**
2 tablespoons **yogurt**
1 dessertspoon **honey**
apple juice

Whizz together and add enough apple juice to bring to a drinking consistency.

Summer fruits

Keep a pack of frozen summer fruits in your freezer.

2 tablespoons **summer fruits**
1 tablespoon of **yogurt**
orange juice or **apple juice**

Whizz together and add enough juice to bring to a drinking consistency.

Salad dressings

I have spoken with a number of students who would like to know how to make some different salad dressings. Making your own saves a heap of money and it is so satisfying. Store any excess in a sealed jar or bottle (or washed out jam jar).

Coconut dressing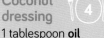

1 tablespoon **oil**

1/2 teaspoon **curry paste**

1/2 mug **coconut milk**

juice of 1/2 **lemon**

1 teaspoon **sugar**

Heat the oil in a small pan, add the curry paste and cook for 30 seconds on a low heat. Take off the heat and mix together with the rest of the ingredients.

French dressing

1 teaspoon **sugar**

1 teaspoon **chives**

juice of 1 **lemon**

2 tablespoons **olive oil**

salt and **pepper**

Mix together, shake if possible.

Creamy paprika dressing

1 teaspoon **sugar**

2 teaspoons **paprika**

4 tablespoons **white wine vinegar**

1 **egg**

3/4 mug **olive oil**

1. Mix everything but the oil together. Using the blender, gradually add the oil. Keep whisking and the dressing should turn thick and creamy.

2. Season with salt and pepper.

Honey and lemon dressing

juice of one **lemon**
2 tablespoons **honey**
1 tablespoon **olive oil**
salt and **pepper**

Mix together, shake if possible.

Peanut dressing

2 tablespoons **peanut butter**
1/3 mug **coconut milk**
1 teaspoon **tomato purée**
1 tablespoon **oil**
1 teaspoon **sugar**

Mix everything together.

Piquant dressing

3 tablespoons **olive oil**
2 tablespoons **white wine vinegar**
1 teaspoon **chopped chives**
1 teaspoon **paprika**
1 tablespoon **soya sauce**
1/4 teaspoon **wholegrain mustard**
3 tablespoons **water**
2 tablespoons **brown sugar**
salt and **pepper**

Mix all ingredients together.

Yogurt dressing

1 small pot of **natural yogurt**
(or 4 tablespoons)
1/2 teaspoon **honey**
grated rind and juice of a **lemon**
2 **spring onions**, finely chopped
salt and **pepper**

Mix everything together.

Raspberry and balsamic dressing

1/3 x 400g pack of **frozen raspberries**, defrosted
4 tablespoons **balsamic vinegar**
4 tablespoons **olive oil**
1 tablespoon **sugar**

1. Push the defrosted raspberries through a sieve.
2. Mix together with the rest of the ingredients.

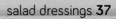

fast food

Home from lectures and in a rush to get out? Here are some quick and easy things for you to try.

Chickpea and Feta Salad

If you want to save half for the next day, divide into 2 portions before adding the dressing, since it causes the greens to wilt.

£0.92 /PERSON

1

2

PREP 10 MINS

Croutons

1 tablespoon **oil** to fry

1 slice **wholemeal bread**

good handful of fresh young **spinach**

1/2 x 400g tin **chickpeas**, rinsed and drained

1/2 x 200g pack of **feta cheese**, cut into chunks

1 medium **red pepper**, roughly chopped

Choose a **dressing** from page 36. Make enough for 2.

1. Prepare a salad dressing. Alternatively, you can use a ready-made French dressing.

2. Make the croutons: heat oil in a frying pan and fry the slice of bread on both sides. Cut into small squares.

3. Sort through the spinach and discard any thick stalks. Put the good spinach in a bowl.

4. Put all the ingredients together in the bowl and mix.

Sweet Potato and Pecan Salad

You can buy portions of celeriac in most supermarkets. Use any leftovers in casseroles, or roast with other vegetables

2 **sweet potatoes**, peeled and diced

French dressing (page 36)

4 **spring onions**, sliced

1 **celery** stick, sliced

½ mug grated **celeriac**

1 teaspoon **chives**

⅓ mug **pecan nuts**

a few **lettuce** leaves

£1.11 /PERSON

2

2

PREP 15 MINS

1. Peel and dice the sweet potato and boil for 10 minutes until tender. Drain and set aside to cool.

2. Make the French dressing.

3. When the sweet potato has cooled, mix in the onions, celery, grated celeriac, chives and pecans.

4. Put the lettuce on a plate and pile the salad on top. Drizzle over the French dressing. Eat straight away.

Pineapple and Pine Nut Salad

If you want to save half for the next day, remember to divide into 2 before adding the dressing.

1 portion of **rice,** cooked (see page 22)

6 florets of **broccoli**

1/2 x 160g pack of **snow peas/sugar snaps**

1 small tin of **pineapple**, drained

1/2 mug **pine nuts**, toasted

1/4 mug **raisins**

2 teaspoons **oil** to fry

Coconut dressing (page 36)

1. Bring half a pan of water to the boil. Add the broccoli to the boiling water and then, 3 minutes later, add the snow peas. Cook for another 3 minutes and both should be cooked.

2. Chop the pineapple into bite-sized pieces.

3. Gently fry the pine nuts in a little oil until they are golden brown.

4. Add all the ingredients together and pour over the coconut dressing.

Ciabatta Goat's Cheese Salad

Goat's cheese is a little more expensive than most cheeses, but has such a unique taste. When combined with ciabatta, it provides an interesting and delicious meal.

£2.34 /PERSON

1

2

PREP 15 MINS

2 tablespoons **olive oil**

1 teaspoon vegetarian **green pesto**

1/2 teaspoon **white wine vinegar**

1 **ciabatta** loaf

4 small **tomatoes**, sliced

125g pack of **goat's cheese**

lettuce

1. Preheat the oven to 220°C fan oven/240°C/Gas 9.

2. Mix the oil, pesto and wine vinegar. Stir well. Cut the bread in two and then take one half and cut horizontally. Leave the other half for tomorrow's sandwiches. Take the 2 halves of bread and sprinkle some of the oil and vinegar over the inside. Place the sliced tomatoes on the bread.

3. Cut the goat's cheese into 6 slices and arrange them over the bread. Brush with dressing and put in the oven for 6 minutes.

4. Pour the remaining dressing over the lettuce and serve together with the bread and cheese.

Green Pesto Pasta with Broccoli

This is a good all-in-one meal. Pasta, broccoli and pine nuts provide a fairly balanced meal. It is also quick and easy to make.

£1.51 /PERSON

1

1

PREP 15 MINS

1 portion of **pasta** (penne is shown in the photo, see page 23)

about 1/2 a head of **broccoli**, broken into small 'trees'

1 dessertspoon **olive oil**

2 tablespoons vegetarian **green pesto**

1 tablespoon **pine nuts**

grated **Parmesan-style cheese** for the top

1. Cook the pasta (see page 23).

2. When the pasta has 5 minutes left to cook, add the broccoli to the saucepan.

3. Drain the pasta and broccoli when cooked.

4. Mix the pesto paste with the oil and the pine nuts. Stir into the pasta and broccoli.

5. Sprinkle the Parmesan over the top and serve.

Cannellini Bean Spaghetti

Very easy, very tasty and very quick. If you freeze half the sauce and beans, you will have a ready-made meal for another day.

£0.59/
PERSON

1

2

PREP
15 MINS

2 portions of **spaghetti** (see page 23)

1 tablespoon **oil** to fry

1 clove **garlic**, chopped

2 **mushrooms**, sliced

400g can **chopped tomatoes**

1/2 mug **water**

1/2 teaspoon **sugar**

1 teaspoon **oregano**

1/2 x 310g can **cannellini beans**, rinsed and drained

12-15 **black olives**

1. Put the spaghetti on to cook (see page 23).

2. Heat the oil in a frying pan. Fry the garlic for 30 seconds, add the mushrooms and cook for 1 minute.

3. Add the rest of the ingredients and simmer for 4–5 minutes. Stir continuously.

4. Drain the pasta and put onto a plate. Pour the bean mixture over the top. Eat!

Joy has more vegetarian recipes at noshbooks.com/veg

Roast Cherry Tomatoes and Spaghetti

Use any leftover feta in a salad or sandwich.

8 **cherry tomatoes**

1 tablespoon **oil** to roast

1 portion of **spaghetti** (see page 23)

12-15 **olives**

1/3 x 200g block of **feta cheese**, cut into chunks

1 teaspoon **chives**

grated **Parmesan-style cheese** (optional)

£1.44 /PERSON

1

1

PREP 5 MINS

COOK 15 MINS

1. Preheat the oven to 180°C fan oven/200°C/Gas 6.

2. Put the tomatoes in an ovenproof dish and drizzle olive oil over them. Season with salt and pepper. Put them in the hot oven to roast for 15 minutes.

3. In the meantime, put the spaghetti on to cook (see page 23).

4. Drain the spaghetti and return to the pan with the olives, feta cheese and chives. When the tomatoes are cooked, tip them and the juices from the bottom of the dish into the pan. Mix together and serve.

Broccoli & Sun-Dried Tomato Pasta

Cooking the spaghetti and broccoli in the same pan saves a bit of washing up.

£1.13 /PERSON

2

1

PREP 20 MINS

1 portion of **spaghetti** (see page 23)

6 small florets of **broccoli**

1 tablespoon **oil** to fry

1/2 **onion**, finely chopped

1 small clove **garlic**, chopped

2 **tomatoes**, cut into chunks

2 **sun-dried tomatoes** cut into slices

salt and **pepper**

grated **Parmesan-style cheese** to serve

1. Put the spaghetti in a pan of boiling water. Cook for 5 minutes. Add the broccoli florets and cook for a further 5 minutes. By this time, both should be cooked.

2. While the spaghetti is cooking, fry the onions and garlic in a frying pan. Cook for 3–4 minutes until the onion begins to brown. Add the tomatoes and sun-dried tomatoes. Cook on a lower heat for another 2–3 minutes. Stir occasionally. Season well with salt and pepper.

3. Drain the pasta and broccoli and mix everything together in the frying pan. This way you will pick up the juices from the frying pan. Serve immediately and top with Parmesan if you wish.

Tagliatelle with Red Pesto

You can add different vegetables to the sauce, such as green beans, mangetout, sugar snaps, etc.

£2.41 /PERSON

2

1

PREP
20 MINS

1 portion of **tagliatelle** (see page 23)

1 tablespoon **oil** to fry

1/2 **onion**, chopped

1/2 **red pepper**, cut into chunks

2 **mushroom**, sliced

1 **tomato**, cut into chunks

1/2 x 190g jar **vegetarian red pesto**

2 tablespoons **cream**

2 tablespoons **pine nuts**

grated **cheese** to serve

1. Cook the tagliatelle (see page 23).
2. Fry the onion, pepper and mushroom for 2 minutes in a frying pan. Add the tomato and cook for 1 minute.
3. Add the pesto, cream and pine nuts and heat through.
4. Drain the tagliatelle and serve the sauce on top. Finish with grated cheese.

Spinach and Cheese Rice Slice

This is a bit like quiche, without the bother of pastry. It is good to eat either hot or cold, therefore it is ideal to make on one day and eat the rest the next day.

£1.84 /PERSON

2

2

PREP 15 MINS

COOK 25 MINS

½ mug long grain **rice**, cooked

1 tablespoon **oil** to fry

1 small **red onion**

100g packet fresh **spinach**

1 mug Cheddar **cheese**

2 tablespoons **cream**

2 **eggs**, beaten

2 **tomatoes**, sliced

½ mug grated **cheese** for the top

1. Preheat the oven to 180°C fan oven/200°C/Gas 6. Grease a small casserole dish.

2. Cook the rice (see page 22).

3. Heat the oil in a frying pan and fry the onions. Once they begin to go soft, add the spinach and cook for 30 seconds or so until it begins to wilt. Take off the heat.

4. Add the cooked rice, cheese, cream and beaten eggs. Season well and stir.

5. Pour into the casserole dish. Arrange the sliced tomatoes on the top. Sprinkle the grated cheese evenly over the top.

6. Cook in the oven for 25 minutes. The cheese should be brown.

Mexican Eggs

This is a good way to use up any leftover tortillas and makes a spicy breakfast alternative, or an interesting snack.

£1.00 /PERSON

2

1

PREP
15 MINS

1 **corn tortilla**

1 tablespoon **oil** to fry

2 **spring onions,** chopped

1 small clove of **garlic,** chopped

3 small pieces **bottled chillies,** chopped

1 **tomato,** cut into chunks

3 **eggs,** beaten

1 teaspoon **chives**

salt and **pepper**

1. Cut the tortilla into strips and fry in oil until golden brown. Set aside.

2. Tip out most of the oil and fry the onions, garlic and chopped chillies for 1 minute. Add the tomatoes and fry for another minute.

3. Add the beaten eggs and chives and stir. Do not overcook the eggs; they need to be quite soft. Season with salt and pepper.

4. Put the tortilla strips on the plate and pour the egg mixture on top.

Potato Pan Cake

You can vary the vegetables but remember to boil them first, see page 20 for timings. This will reheat, but best shared.

£1.22 /PERSON

3

2

PREP 25 MINS

2 medium **potatoes**, diced

1 small **carrot**, chopped

a few florets of **broccoli**

1 tablespoon **oil** to fry

1 small **onion**, chopped

1 clove **garlic**, chopped

2 **tomatoes**, cut into chunks

1/2 x 200g pack of **feta cheese** or 1/2 x 390g **pack tofu**

salt and **pepper**

1 mug grated **Cheddar cheese**

1. Put the potatoes and the carrots in boiling water, simmer for 5 minutes, then add the broccoli. Cook for a further 5 minutes until everything is tender.

2. Turn the grill on to heat up.

3. Heat a little oil in the frying pan and fry the onions, garlic and tomatoes in a frying pan. Allow them to brown a little. Add the drained potatoes, broccoli and carrots. Fry together for 2–3 minutes. Stir in the tofu or the feta cheese and season.

4. Sprinkle over the grated cheese and put under the hot grill until the cheese browns. Be careful not to push the pan in too far, or the handle will burn. Serve immediately.

Quick Veggie Pasta

Quick, easy and inexpensive meal to make. You can obviously vary the veggies; try peppers, baby sweetcorn, mangetout, etc.

£0.99 /PERSON

1

2

PREP 20 MINS

1 tablespoon **oil** to fry

1 small **onion**, sliced

1 clove **garlic**, finely chopped

1 small **courgette**, cut into small pieces

4 **mushrooms**, sliced

10 **olives**, roughly chopped

4 **cherry tomatoes**, cut in half

Dressing

2 tablespoons **balsamic vinegar**

2 tablespoons **olive oil**

2 teaspoons **sugar**

salt and **pepper**

spaghetti or **tagliatelle** (see page 23)

Parmesan-style cheese to serve

1. Mix together the dressing ingredients. Set to one side.
2. Put the pasta on to cook (see page 23).
3. Heat the oil in a wok. Add the onions, garlic and courgettes and fry until they begin to brown.
4. Add the mushrooms and fry for 1–2 minutes. season well.
5. Add the tomatoes and take off the heat. There will be enough heat in the pan to warm them. If you cook them too much, they will go mushy.
6. Add the drained pasta and olives. Stir.
7. Serve in pasta bowls and drizzle the dressing over. Grate some Parmesan cheese over the top.

Salad Tortillas with Feta

Use the leftover feta in another salad or sandwiches (see page 26).

£1.10 /PERSON

2

2

PREP 15 MINS

2–3 corn **tortilla wraps**

2–3 tablespoons **crème fraîche**

1 **little gem lettuce**, cut horizontally

2 **tomatoes**, sliced

7cm piece of **cucumber**, cut into long strips

3 **spring onions**, cut lengthways into strips

10 **olives**

1/2 x 200g pack of **feta cheese**

salt and **pepper**

1. Heat the tortillas under the grill for 30 seconds.

2. Spread a tablespoon of crème fraîche on each tortilla.

3. Divide the lettuce, tomatoes, cucumber, spring onions and olives between the tortillas.

4. Cut the feta cheese into cubes and divide between the tortillas. Season well.

5. Roll up the tortillas and cut in half. Serve.

Thai Coconut Veggies

Good to heat up next day.

£0.81 /PERSON

1

4

PREP 30MINS

1 **carrot**, cut into bite-sized chunks

1 **sweet potato**, cut into 2cm cubes

1 **potato**, cut into 2cm cubes

1/2 x 200g pack **green beans**, each cut in half

1 small head **broccoli**, broken into small trees

1 tablespoon **oil** to fry

1 **onion**, cut into v

1/2 **red pepper**, cut into chunks

1 tablespoon **Thai red curry paste**

400 ml can **coconut milk**

pilau rice to serve (see page 22)

1. Put some water in a pan to boil for the veggies. Once boiling, add the carrots, sweet potatoes and potatoes. Simmer gently for 5 minutes. Add the broccoli and beans and simmer for a further 5 minutes. Drain and return to the pan until needed.

2. Heat a little oil in a wok and fry the onions and the peppers until they become soft.

3. Add the curry paste and fry for 30 seconds.

4. Add the coconut milk and the cooked vegetables and simmer for 5 minutes.

5. Serve with the rice (see page 22).

broke but hungry

Waiting for pay day, or is the loan rapidly running out? Here are some inexpensive dishes to keep the hunger pangs at bay.

French Onion Soup

You can use these cheesy croutons with other soups, as they will make more of a whole meal.

£0.72 /PERSON

1½ tablespoons **oil** to fry

1 large **onion**, sliced

1½ mugs **water** + 1 **vegetable stock** cube

½ teaspoon **Marmite**

salt and **pepper**

Cheesy Croutons

1 slice **wholemeal bread**

¼ mug grated **cheese**

PREP 20 MINS

COOK 10 MINS

1. Heat the oil in a saucepan. Add the sliced onions. Fry on a fairly high heat for 6–8 minutes until the onions are really brown, but not burned. You will need to watch them carefully and stir frequently to stop them from actually burning.

2. Once the onions are really brown, add the water, crumbled stock cube and Marmite. Bring to the boil and then turn down to simmer for 5 minutes.

3. While the soup is cooking, make some cheese on toast (see page 28). You will not need to butter the toast. Once toasted, cut into squares to use as croutons.

4. Taste the soup and season. Pour into a bowl and drop the croutons on top.

Tomato and Lentil Soup

Use a hand-held blender for this recipe. If you don't have one, don't worry. It tastes just the same unblended. Make enough for 2 and eat the rest the next day.

£0.66 /PERSON

2

2

PREP 15 MINS

COOK 20 MINS

1 tablespoon **oil** to fry

1 medium **onion**, chopped

1 medium **carrot**, chopped

1 clove **garlic**, chopped

1/4 mug **red lentils**

400g can **tomatoes**

1/2 teaspoon **Marmite**

11/2 mug **water** + 1 **vegetable stock cube**, crumbled in

bread to serve

1. Heat a little oil in a saucepan and add the onions, carrots and garlic. Cook until the onions are soft.

2. Add the lentils, tomatoes, Marmite, stock cube and water. Bring to the boil, then turn down and simmer for 20 minutes until the lentils are tender.

3. Once the soup is cooked, season well with salt and freshly ground black pepper. Use a hand-held blender to blitz the soup. Serve with bread.

Apple and Cashew Soup

This soup is quick and easy to make. Make enough for 2 and you can keep the rest for the next day. Alternatively, freeze it and keep for a day when you are too busy to cook.

£0.66 /PERSON

2

2

PREP 10 MINS

COOK 20 MINS

1 tablespoon **oil** to fry

2 **carrots**, sliced

1 small **onion**, chopped

1 small **potato**, cut into chunks

1 **eating apple**, peeled and cut into chunks

1¹/₂ mugs **water**

1 **vegetable stock cube**, crumbled

¹/₄ x 100g pack of **cashews**, chopped

salt and **pepper**

1. Heat a little oil in a saucepan and fry the carrots, onion, potatoes and apple in the oil. Allow the vegetables to brown a little.

2. Add the rest of the ingredients and bring to the boil. Simmer for 20 minutes until the vegetables are tender.

3. Allow to cool a little, then whizz with the blender. Reheat and season well with salt and pepper.

Sweetcorn Soup

Use the rest of the tin of sweetcorn in a risotto or salad.

1 tablespoon **oil** to fry

1/2 onion, chopped

1 **pepper**, red or green, cut into strips

1 mug of **water**

1 **vegetable stock cube**, crumbled

1/2 x 340g can of **sweetcorn**, drained

1 tablespoon **double cream**

salt and **pepper**

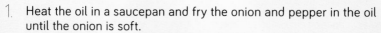

1. Heat the oil in a saucepan and fry the onion and pepper in the oil until the onion is soft.

2. Add the water and stock cube and bring to the boil. Add the sweetcorn and simmer for 3–4 minutes.

3. Whiz the soup with the blender, but do not make it too fine; keep it a bit lumpy. Stir in the cream and season with salt and pepper.

Lentil and Apricot Soup

Ready-to-eat dried apricots are usually found in the 'baking section' at the supermarket and make great, healthy snacks.

3 tablespoons **red lentils**

1 tablespoon chopped ready-to-eat **dried apricots**

1 medium **potato**, diced

2 mugs **water** + 2 **vegetable stock** cubes, crumbled in

juice of half a **lemon**

1 teaspoon **curry paste**

1 teaspoon **oregano**

salt and **pepper**

£0.45 /PERSON

1

2

PREP
10 MINS

COOK
30 MINS

1. Put all the ingredients, except the oregano, in a saucepan. Bring to the boil, then turn down the heat and simmer for 30 minutes.

2. Whizz with the hand-held blender. Add the oregano. Season well. Reheat and serve.

Apple and Bean Salad

You can use any variety of canned beans. Always be sure to rinse them well, as some of the soaking juices are not good for you.

£0.91 /PERSON

2

2-3

PREP 20 MINS

2 medium **potatoes**, diced

1 **red dessert apple**

400g can of **barlotti beans**, or any other canned beans (not baked beans!)

2 **spring onions**, chopped

1 small **yellow pepper**, diced

Dressing

juice of a **lemon**

2 tablespoons **olive oil**

1 dessertspoon **wholegrain mustard**

1 **clove garlic**, chopped

1 teaspoon **sugar**

1 teaspoon **chives**

salt and **pepper**

1. Boil the diced potatoes for 10–15 minutes until they are cooked. Drain.
2. Peel the apple, remove the core and chop into chunks.
3. Mix together the beans, apple, spring onions and pepper.
4. Mix together the dressing ingredients and drizzle over the top of the salad.
5. Serve with green salad.

Potato Hash

So quick and easy. This is a good way to liven-up a potato and half a tin of beans. Serve with tomato ketchup or HP sauce.

£0.95 /PERSON

2

1

PREP 25 MINS

2 medium potatoes

½ x 400g tin **baked beans**

1 tablespoon **oil** to fry

½ mug grated **Cheddar cheese**

1. Dice the potatoes and boil for 10 minutes until cooked. Drain, return to the pan and squash them a little with a fork. Do not mash them.

2. Stir in the beans.

3. Heat some oil in a frying pan and tip the mixture in. Don't stir, allow it to fry and brown on the bottom. Once browned, using a slotted turner, stir all the browned bits up from the bottom, leave again to allow the rest to brown. Stir in the browned bits again.

4. Serve on a plate and put the grated cheese on the top, whilst it is still hot, so that it melts. Add some ketchup or HP.

Channa Dhal

This dish makes a meal in itself, or can be eaten with bread, naan bread, rice, or jacket potatoes. Use up any leftover coconut milk in a salad dressing or sauce (see pages 36 or 33).

£0.58 /PERSON

1

2-3

PREP 15 MINS

1 tablespoon **oil** to fry

1 small **onion**, finely chopped

2 **cloves garlic**, chopped finely

¹/₂ teaspoon freshly grated **ginger**

1 tablespoon **curry paste**

¹/₂ x 400g can **tomatoes**

2 tablespoons **coconut milk**

400g tin of **chickpeas**

salt and **pepper**

1. Heat the oil in a frying pan and fry the onions and garlic until they begin to brown. Stir frequently. Once brown, add the ginger and curry paste. Cook for 1 minute.

2. Add the tomatoes, coconut milk and chickpeas. Season well with salt and pepper. Cook for about 5 minutes until the mixture begins to thicken.

Bean Burgers

If you want to keep one of the burgers for the next day, don't fry it, but wrap it in cling film and keep it in the fridge.

£ 0.73 /PERSON

3

2-3

PREP 30 MINS

1/2 x 750g pack of frozen **broad beans**

1 **egg**, beaten

1 slice **bread**, made into breadcrumbs

1 small **onion**, grated

1 bag **ready salted crisps**, crushed

1 tablespoon **oil** to fry

Toppings

1 **onion**, sliced

pickles, e.g. gherkins

tomato sauce

1. Allow the beans to defrost. Mash with a fork, or whizz a little with the blender. Don't make them too pulpy, leave a bit of texture.

2. Put the egg and breadcrumbs in a bowl and allow the bread to soak up the egg. Mix well. Add the beans.

3. Grate the onions and squeeze out most of the liquid. Add to the bean mixture and mix well.

4. Shape the mixture into 2–3 burgers. Put the crushed crisps on a plate and roll the burgers in them.

5. Heat oil in a frying pan and cook the burgers for about 5 minutes each side. Take care that they do not burn. If they brown before the 5 minutes, just turn them and turn down the heat. They will need a total of 10 minutes in order to be heated through.

6. While they are cooking, slice the other onion (for the toppings) and fry in a saucepan until caramelised (i.e. really brown). You will need to stir them frequently.

7. Slice the burger bun in half, horizontally. Put the burger inside, with the onions on top and some tomato sauce and pickle to finish. Enjoy!

Greek Style Egg Curry

This recipe is quite spicy. You can vary the type and amount of curry paste you use. Stirring in the yogurt makes the curry milder.

£0.894 /PERSON

3

2

PREP 30 MINS

1 tablespoon **oil** to fry

1 medium **onion**, sliced

230g can of **chopped tomatoes**

1/2 mug **frozen peas**

1 dessertspoon **curry paste**

4 **eggs**

2 tablespoons **Greek yogurt**

to serve

rice (see page 22)

mango chutney

1. Heat the oil in a frying pan, add the onion and cook for 5 minutes until it begins to go brown. Stir frequently. Add the tomatoes, peas and curry paste. Bring to the boil, then simmer for 20 minutes.

2. Meanwhile, put the eggs on to boil for 8 minutes. When cooked, run cold water over them and then peel. Cut each egg in half.

3. Gently stir them into the curry. Add the yogurt, serve with rice (see page 22) and mango chutney.

Spicy Potato Cakes

You can make these potato cakes with or without the spice, depending on your taste, just leave out the chillies. Serve with baked beans, spicy chickpeas (page 84), or salsa (see page 147).

£0.65 /PERSON

2

2

PREP 25 MINS

2 large **potatoes**, diced

4 or 5 pieces of **pickled jalapeño** or hot sweet chillies, chopped

1/2 mug grated **Cheddar cheese**

2 teaspoons chopped **chives**

2 spring **onions**, chopped

salt and **pepper**

1/2 beaten **egg**

1 tablespoon **oil** to fry

salsa (page 147)

1. Put the potatoes in boiling water and simmer for about 10 minutes until they are cooked. Mash lightly with a fork.

2. Add the chillies, cheese, chives, spring onions, salt and pepper and just enough egg to make everything stick together. If you add too much egg, it will be difficult to fry. Form the mixture into 4 potato cakes.

3. Heat a little oil in a frying pan. Fry the potato cakes on each side for about 4–5 minutes until they are browned.

4. Serve with the salsa.

Baked Patties with Chilli Sauce

Baking in the oven gives a 'roasted' flavour. If you have a little cream handy, make the spicy sauce to go with them. If not, make one of the sauces on pages 32 & 33.

£1.15 /PERSON

3

2

PREP 15 MINS

COOK 25 MINS

1 medium **potato**, diced
1/2 an **onion**, grated
1 small **carrot**, grated
1/4 mug grated **Parmesan-style cheese**
1 **courgette**, grated
1 stick **celery**, finely

chopped
1/2 teaspoon **oregano**
1 vegetable **stock cube**
1 beaten **egg**
oil
salt and pepper

Chilli sauce

1/2 mug **cream**
1/2 vegetable **stock cube**, crumbled
1/4 teaspoon **chilli flakes**
1/2 teaspoon **oregano**.

1. Preheat the oven to 180°C fan oven/200°C/Gas 6.

2. Boil the potatoes for about 10 minutes until they are soft. Drain well and mash with a fork. Add the grated onion, carrot, cheese, courgette, celery, and oregano. Crumble the stock cube over and mix. Add the egg a little at a time, taking care that the mixture does not get too soft. You will probably only need half the egg.

3. Grease a baking tray and pile the mixture into 3–4 piles. Shape into rounds. Cook in the oven for 25 minutes; the patties should go slightly brown.

4. To make the sauce, simply put all the ingredients in a pan and heat. Do not boil.

Quorn Madras Curry

It's quite a good idea to keep a packet of Quorn in your freezer drawer.

1 tablespoon **oil** to fry

1/2 x 350g packet of **Quorn chicken-style** pieces

1 small **onion**, chopped

1 small **sweet potato**, peeled and cut into small chunks

1 **clove garlic**

1 tablespoon **Madras curry paste**

400g tin **chopped tomatoes**

1 mug **water** + 1 vegetable **stock cube**, crumbled

1 tablespoon **raisins**

rice to serve (see page 22)

£1.10 /PERSON

1

2-3

PREP 35 MINS

1. Heat the oil in a wok and fry the Quorn, onions, sweet potatoes and garlic until they all begin to brown.

2. Add the curry paste to the pan and cook for 30 seconds.

3. Add the rest of the ingredients. Simmer gently for 15–20 minutes.

4. Serve with rice (see page 22).

one-pot dishes

Tired of washing up loads of pots and pans? These one-pot dishes will minimise the clearing-up process.

one pot dishes

Biryani with Yogurt and Cashews

Try not to stir too much in stage 3 as the rice will become mushy.

£0.94 /PERSON

3

4

PREP 35 MINS

50g **butter**, measure by pack

1 medium **onion**, cut into wedges

2 tablespoons **Korma curry paste**

1 mug **rice**

1 dessertspoon **liquid vegetable stock** or a stock cube

1 mug **Greek yogurt**

1 small **cauliflower**, cut into florets

1 mug **frozen peas**

1/2 mug **raisins**

100g pack **cashews**

1 teaspoon **turmeric**

2 mugs **water**

naan breads

1. Heat the butter in a large pan or wok and cook the onions until they become soft. Add the Korma paste and turmeric and cook for 1 minute.

2. Add the rice and stir well. Cook for 1 minute, allowing the rice to absorb the flavours.

3. Add the stock, yogurt, cauliflower, peas, raisins, cashews, and water. Bring to the boil. Turn down the heat to low and simmer with the lid on (you can use foil if the wok does not have a lid) for 25 minutes. Check every 10 minutes to make sure it is not sticking to the bottom. You may need to add a little more water. Serve with warm naan breads.

Sweet Potato Tagine

You could also eat this with rice, potatoes or crusty bread.

£0.89 /PERSON

2

4

PREP 30 MINS

2 tablespoons **oil** to fry

1 **onion**, chopped

2 cloves **garlic**, finely chopped

2 teaspoons ground **coriander**

2 teaspoons **cumin**

2 teaspoons **paprika**

1 small **aubergine**, cut into cubes

2 small **sweet potatoes**, peeled and cut into cubes

400g tin **chopped tomatoes**

1 mug **water**

6 ready-to-eat dried **apricots**, chopped

2 teaspoons **sugar**

1/2 mug **raisins**

1/2 x 400g tin **chickpeas**, washed and drained

1 **courgette**, cut into chunks

1 tablespoon **tomato purée**

2 mugs of **couscous**

4 mugs **water** + 1 vegetable **stock cube**

1. Heat the oil in a wok or large saucepan. Add the onions and garlic and fry until the onions are soft.

2. Add the coriander, cumin and paprika and fry for 30 seconds.

3. Add the aubergines and the sweet potatoes to the wok and fry for 1 minute. Stir frequently.

4. Add the tin of tomatoes, water, apricots, sugar, raisins and chickpeas. Bring to the boil and then simmer gently, for 10 minutes. Cover with a lid or some foil.

5. Add the courgettes and the tomato purée and simmer for a further 5 minutes.

6. While the tagine is cooking, put the couscous in a bowl and add the boiling water and stock cube. Cover with a plate and leave to stand for 5 minutes until all the water is absorbed.

7. Serve the tagine on the couscous.

Fancy a bit more spice? Why not try Joy's Saffron Vegetable Tagine. You can find her recipe at noshbooks.com/saffron

Leek and Potato Frittata with Salad

Frittata is a good way of making a meal in one pan. You can add many different kinds of things, for example, tomatoes or mushrooms.

£0.95 /PERSON

1

4

PREP 30 MINS

1 large **potato,** cut into 2cm cubes

oil for roasting

50g **butter** to fry, measure by packet

2 small **leeks**, cut into slices

6 large **eggs**, beaten

200g block of **feta cheese**, cubed

2 teaspoons **dried basil**

1 mug grated **Cheddar cheese**

Piquant Tomato Sauce to serve (see page 32)

salad to serve

---

1. Preheat the oven to 200°C fan oven/220°C/Gas 7.

2. Put the cubed potatoes on a baking tray, sprinkle with oil. Season well and distribute the oil evenly with your hands. Place in the oven for 20 minutes until they are browned.

3. Preheat the grill.

4. Heat the butter in a frying pan and add the leeks. Cook until they are tender.

5. Beat the eggs in a bowl, then add to the frying pan. Cook for 1 minute or until the egg at the bottom of the pan begins to set. Gently move the egg around in the pan to allow the runny egg to get to the bottom of the pan.

6. Add the cooked potatoes, feta cheese and the basil. Sprinkle the Cheddar cheese over the top.

7. Place under the grill for 5–10 minutes until the cheese browns and the egg is set.

8. Serve with the tomato sauce.

We love fritattas. Not only are they easy and tasty, you also don't have much washing up to do. Try Joy's Spaghetti Fritatta at noshbooks.com/fritatta

Roast Sweet Potatoes with Couscous and Balsamic Dressing

Roasting vegetables is so easy and enhances the flavours. If you use other veggies, remember to cut small the ones which take the longest to cook (see page 21).

£1.58 /PERSON

1

2

PREP
15 MINS

COOK
25 MINS

1 **sweet potato**, peeled and cut into small chunks

1 **red pepper**, cut into large chunks

1 **courgette**, cut into slices

1 **onion**, cut into wedges

2 cloves **garlic**, left whole

2 tablespoons **olive oil**

1 teaspoon **dried rosemary**

³/4 mug **couscous**

1¹/2 mugs boiling **water** + vegetable **stock cube**

400g can **black-eyed beans**, drained and rinsed

Dressing

2 tablespoons **balsamic vinegar**

2 tablespoons **olive oil**

2 teaspoons **sugar**

salt and **pepper**

---

1. Preheat the oven to 200°C fan oven/220°C/Gas 7.

2. Place the sweet potato, pepper, courgette, onion and garlic on a baking tray. Season well with salt and pepper. Sprinkle with the olive oil and mix everything together well to distribute the oil evenly. Sprinkle the rosemary over the top and place in the oven for 20 minutes until the veggies are browned.

3. While the veggies are in the oven, put the couscous in a bowl and pour over the boiling water and stir in the stock cube. Cover the bowl and leave until all the water is absorbed.

4. Mix together the dressing ingredients.

5. Simmer the beans in a little water for 1 minute and then drain.

6. Once the veggies are cooked, mix together with the beans. Drizzle over the dressing.

7. Serve with the couscous.

Korma Rice and Spinach

If you like your food spicy, add an extra tablespoon of curry paste or use a hotter paste like Madras. Recipe just uses a wok, so not too much washing up here.

£2.03 /PERSON

2

2

PREP 30 MINS

1 tablespoon **oil** to fry

1 **onion**, sliced

1 clove **garlic**, chopped finely

1 tablespoon **Korma curry paste**

2 **tomatoes**, chopped

1/2 mug basmati **rice**

1 mug **water** + 1 vegetable **stock** cube

1/2 x 400g tin **chickpeas**, washed and drained

1/2 mug **raisins**

1/2 x 100g pack **pine nuts**

1/2 x 200g pack of fresh **spinach**

crème fraîche or natural **yogurt** to serve

1. Heat a little oil in a wok. Add the onions and garlic and fry until soft.

2. Add the curry paste and tomatoes and fry for 30 seconds. Add the uncooked rice and cook for a further 30 seconds.

3. Add the stock and water and bring to the boil.

4. Add the chickpeas and the raisins. Turn down to simmer for 10–15 minutes until most of the water has been absorbed.

5. Add the pine nuts and the fresh spinach. Stir until the spinach is wilted. Should only take 30 seconds or so.

6. Serve with a little yogurt.

Sweet Potato and Coconut Curry

Keep a couple of naan breads in the freezer as they freeze quite well.

£1.67 /PERSON

2

2-3

PREP 35 MINS

1 tablespoon **oil** to fry

1 **onion**, cut into thin wedges

2 **sweet potatoes**, peeled and cut into bite-sized chunks

3 tablespoons **red lentils**

1 vegetable **stock cube**

400g can **coconut milk**

1 **courgette**, cut into bite-sized pieces

1/2 mug **frozen peas**

1/2 x 200g pack **green beans**

2 tablespoons **Korma** or **tandoori curry paste**

rice to serve (see page 22)

1. Heat the oil in a frying pan or wok. Add the onions and cook until they begin to soften. Add the curry paste and cook for 1 minute.

2. Add the lentils, sweet potato, green beans, coconut milk, water and stock cube. Bring to the boil. Turn down and simmer, without a lid, for 10 -12 minutes until the sweet potato is tender and the lentils softened. Stir occasionally.

3. Add the courgette and the peas. Simmer for another 5–6 minutes. Stir occasionally.

4. While the curry is cooking, make the rice (see page 22).

5. Serve the curry with the rice or naan bread.

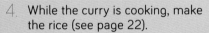

Basic Risotto

Risotto is a very versatile recipe. The instructions below give you the basic idea and then you can experiment and add different ingredients yourself. Arborio rice is the best to use for risotto, but you can use long grain or other varieties.

£2.44 /PERSON

2

1

PREP 10 MINS

COOK 30 MINS

1 tablespoon **oil** to fry

1/2 **onion**, chopped

1 clove of **garlic**, chopped

1/2 mug **Arborio/risotto rice**

11/2 mugs **water**

1 vegetable **stock cube**

1 **leek**, sliced

1/2 **courgette**, cut into small pieces.

2 **mushrooms**, sliced

1 tablespoon **pine nuts**

salt and **pepper**

1. Heat the oil in a frying pan and fry the onions and garlic for 1 minute. Add the rice and fry for another minute.

2. Add the water, crumbled stock cube, leeks, courgette and mushrooms. Bring to the boil and season well with salt and pepper.

3. Simmer, with a lid on the pan (use foil if no lid), for 25-30 minutes until the rice is tender and the liquid is almost gone. Risotto should not be really dry. Don't allow all the liquid to boil away. Add more liquid if necessary.

4. Add the pine nuts at the end of the cooking time. Season well.

Variations on Risotto

Here are a few ideas for variations on the basic risotto recipe. If you are using vegetables which cook in a short time, they need to be added towards the end of the cooking time. Broccoli is not great in risotto, because it tends to break up and go mushy. These variations begin at stage 2 of the basic recipe. So, always begin with the onions, garlic and rice and water.

Green Veg Risotto

At stage 2, add green beans, cut into pieces, peas and broad beans.

At the end of the cooking time, add some spinach and cook until it wilts.

Serve topped with grated Parmesan-style cheese.

Spicy Pumpkin Risotto

At stage 2, add 1 small deseeded chilli, chopped, a vegetable stock cube, pieces of pumpkin or squash, half a courgette, chopped, and 2 sliced mushrooms.

At the end of the cooking time, top with grated Cheddar cheese; it will melt into the risotto. Don't try to cook the cheese or stir it in.

Green Pepper and Sweetcorn Risotto

At stage 2, add half a green pepper, roughly chopped and a sliced mushroom.

5 minutes before the end of the cooking time, add a small tin of sweetcorn and a tablespoon of cashew nuts.

Spicy Bean Risotto

At stage 2, add 1 tablespoon black-eyed beans, either tinned or soaked, 1 carrot, chopped, 1 small courgette, chopped, 2 teaspoons curry paste and some chives.

Mexican Risotto

At stage 2, replace 1 mug of water with 1/2 a 400g tin of chopped tomatoes.

Also add, 1 chopped red pepper, 1 deseeded red chilli, chopped, half a tin of chickpeas and a teaspoon of sugar.

Serve topped with grated Cheddar cheese, or with soured cream.

Spanish Risotto

At stage 2, replace the 1 mug of water with 1/2 a 400g tin of chopped tomatoes.

Also, add 2 sliced mushrooms and 1/2 a chopped, red pepper.

5 minutes before the end, add 6–8 olives.

Serve topped with a fried egg.

Basic Stir-fry

Stir-fry is something of a staple dish for vegetarian students. Here is a basic method, plus a few variations for you to work on. If you want to use root vegetables (potatoes, carrots, parsnips, swedes, etc.), you will need to precook them (see page 20). Pictured opposite is ginger and corn stir-fry.

£2.12 /PERSON

2

1

PREP 25 MINS

1 tablespoon **oil** to fry

1 clove **garlic**, chopped

1 teaspoon freshly grated **ginger**

2 **spring onions**, chopped

6 pieces **baby sweetcorn**, cut in half

1/2 red **pepper**, sliced

6 **sugar snaps** or **mangetout**

1/2 mug **water** with 1 vegetable **stock cube**, crumbled

2 tablespoons **soy sauce**

5cm piece of **courgette**, sliced

3 small florets of **broccoli**

salt and **pepper**

1/2 x 200g pack of **ready-to-use noodles**

1. Heat the oil in a wok. If you do not have one, a frying pan is fine. Fry the garlic, ginger and onion for 1–2 minutes, then add the rest of the ingredients, apart from the noodles. Keep the heat high and cook for 4–5 minutes until the vegetables are cooked and almost all of the liquid has reduced. You can cover with a lid or some foil.

2. Stir in the noodles. Heat for 1 minute.

3. Season well with salt and pepper and eat straight away.

Stir-fry variations

Stir-frying is easy. To avoid overcooked vegetables, use only a small amount of water, stock, or sauce. Cut the vegetables up quite small: this looks better and cooks quicker. Cook the onions and garlic first, then add the other ingredients. Soy sauce, chilli sauce, hoisin sauce, etc., are great to use. Keep a few of these sauces in your storecupboard.

Tomato with vegetables

1/2 an **onion**, chopped finely

1 clove **garlic**, finely chopped

1 **courgette**, sliced

1/2 a **pepper**, sliced

2 slices of **aubergine**

2 **mushrooms**, sliced

1 tablespoon **oil** to fry

1. Fry all the ingredients first in a little oil.
2. Add 1/2 tin of **chopped tomatoes**, and 1 teaspoon of **HP sauce.**
3. Cook for 3-4 minutes.
4. Add noodles.

Spinach

2 sliced **spring onions**

1 clove of **garlic,** finely chopped

1/2 **red pepper**, thinly sliced

1 teaspoon **soy sauce**

1 teaspoon **honey**

1/2 mug **water**

handful of **spinach**

2 tablespoons of **nuts**

1. Fry the onions garlic and peppers.
2. Add the water, soy and honey, heat for 30 seconds.
3. Add the spinach and nuts, heat for 30 seconds.

Bean sprouts and vegetables

2 **spring onions**, chopped

1 clove **garlic**, chopped

1 sliced **pepper**

1 sliced **courgette**

2 sliced **mushrooms**

6 **sugar snaps**

1 teaspoon **soy sauce**

1 teaspoon **sugar**

1/2 mug **water**

handful of **bean sprouts**

1 tablespoon **pine nuts**

1. Fry the onions, garlic, peppers and courgettes for 2-3 minutes.
2. Add the mushrooms, sugar snaps, water, soy and sugar. Cook for 1 minute.
3. Add the bean sprouts and pine nuts and cook for 30 seconds.

Creamy vegetables

1 tablespoon **oil** to fry

1 small, chopped **onion**

1 finely chopped **carrot**

2 thin slices of **aubergine**

2 sliced **mushrooms**

1/2 green **pepper**, sliced or chopped

1/2 vegetable **stock cube**, crumbled + 1/2 mug **water**

2 tablespoons of **double cream**

1. Fry the onions, carrot and aubergine for 2–3 minutes.
2. Add the peppers and mushrooms. Cook for 1 minute.
3. Add the rest of the ingredients and cook until heated through.

Cashews and vegetables

firm **tofu** (1/4 pack)

1 teaspoon **hoisin sauce**

1 tablespoon **cashews**

1/2 chopped **pepper**

1 clove **garlic**, chopped

2 **spring onions,** chopped

6–8 **sugar snaps**

1/2 vegetable **stock cube** (crumbled) + 1/2 mug **water**

handful of **bean sprouts**

1. Fry the onion garlic and peppers for 2 minutes.
2. Add the sugar snaps, hoisin, water and stock, cook for 1 minute.
3. Add the bean sprouts and tofu and heat through.

Other things to use as sauces:

coconut milk mixed with a teaspoon of **curry paste**

chilli sauce

tomato sauce

vegetable stock

Other things to add to stir-fry:

egg noodles: a handful per person

rice noodles: a handful per person

rice: (see page 22)

omelette strips: to make these, beat an **egg** and before you start cooking the vegetables, put a little oil in the pan, pour in the egg and spread it around the pan, just like a pancake. Cook until it is brown on one side, then turn it over. When cooked, take out of the pan and cut into strips. Add to the stir-fry at the end. Use 1 egg per person.

fried tortilla wraps: fry and cut into strips and add at the end to keep them crisp. Use 1 **tortilla** per person.

Spicy Chickpeas with Spinach

Chickpeas are high in protein and inexpensive. Good to reheat the next day. Serve with jacket potatoes, or rice, and yogurt.

1 tablespoon **oil** to fry

1/2 **red onion**, chopped

2 **tomatoes**, chopped

1 dessertspoon **curry paste**

2/3 mug **water** + 1 vegetable **stock cube**

400g can **chickpeas**, drained and rinsed

1/4 x 200g pack of **spinach**

1 mug grated **cheese**

salt and **pepper**

yogurt to serve

£1.73 /PERSON

2

2

PREP 15 MINS

COOK 10 MINS

1. Heat the oil in a saucepan and fry the onion until it becomes soft.
2. Add the tomatoes, curry paste, water, crumbled stock cube and chickpeas. Bring to the boil and then simmer for about 10 minutes.
3. Add the spinach and stir until it wilts, about 30 seconds.
4. Take off the heat and stir in the cheese which will melt. Season with salt and pepper.
5. Serve with jacket potatoes (page 24), or rice (see page 22), and yogurt.

Quorn Chilli with Aduki Beans

This is good to reheat the next day. Aduki beans are a bit more tender than red kidney beans, but you can use either.

£1.04 /PERSON

2

4

PREP 25 MINS

1 tablespoon **oil** to fry

1 **onion**, chopped

1 clove **garlic**, finely chopped

350g packet of **Quorn mince**

1 tin **red kidney beans** or **aduki beans**

400g tin **tomatoes**

6 **mushrooms**, sliced

2 teaspoons **chilli powder**

2 tablespoons **tomato purée**

1/2 mug **water**

1 teaspoon **sugar**

rice (see page 22) or **bread** to serve

1. Heat the oil in a wok or large saucepan and fry the onions and garlic until the onions are soft.

2. Add the rest of the ingredients, bring to the boil, then turn down to simmer for 10–15 minutes.

3. Serve with crusty bread or rice (see page 22).

Squash and Apple Curry

Serve with yogurt, naan bread and rice. Use the rest of the butternut squash to make soup. Use the Leek Soup recipe on page 155, replacing the potato and carrot with the butternut squash.

1 tablespoon **oil** to fry

1 small **onion**, chopped

2 large **potatoes**, diced

1/2 **butternut squash**, peeled and cut into small chunks

1 eating **apple**, cored and chopped into chunks

1 mug **water**

1 vegetable **stock cube**

1 tablespoon **raisins**

1 teaspoon **curry paste**

naan bread, **rice** (see page 22) and **yogurt** to serve

£1.04 /PERSON

1

2

PREP 30 MINS

COOK 20 MINS

1. Heat the oil in a saucepan. Add the onions, potatoes and squash and fry for 5 minutes until they begin to brown.

2. Add the apple, water, crumbled stock cube, raisins and curry paste. Bring to the boil. Turn down the heat, put the lid on the pan and simmer for 15–20 minutes until the vegetables are cooked.

Aubergine and Coconut Curry

You can add other vegetables to this recipe, just remember to allow enough simmering time for the vegetables to cook. Use the timings on page 20 as a guide.

£1.36 /PERSON

2

2

PREP 15 MINS

COOK 15 MINS

1 tablespoon **oil** to fry

1 **onion**, sliced

1 clove **garlic**, chopped

1 teaspoon freshly grated **ginger**

1 tablespoon **curry paste**

1 **aubergine**, sliced

400ml can **coconut milk**

rice (see page 22) and **yogurt** to serve

1. Fry the onions, garlic and ginger in a saucepan. When the onions begin to brown, add the curry paste and coconut milk.

2. Bring to the boil and then add the aubergines.

3. Simmer for 15 minutes until the aubergine is soft.

4. Serve with rice (see page 22) and yogurt.

something mum might cook

Missing home and never thought you would? Here are a few ideas to remind you of your mum's cooking.

Pasta with Roast Vegetables

Roasting vegetables is so easy and creates a delicious flavour as the starches in the vegetables caramelise (see page 21 for roasting other vegetables).

£0.78 /PERSON

2

2

PREP 15 MINS

COOK 30 MINS

1/2 **onion**, cut into wedges

1 **courgette**, cut into wedges

1 clove **garlic**, chopped

1 tablespoon **oil** to roast

3-4 **cherry tomatoes**

2 **mushrooms**, sliced

salt and **pepper**

1 portion of **pasta** (see page 23)

1. Preheat the oven to 200°C fan oven/240°C/Gas 7.

2. Put the onion, courgette, chopped garlic, cherry tomatoes and mushrooms on a baking tray. Sprinkle on the oil and some salt and pepper. Toss the vegetables in the oil and seasoning so it is evenly distributed.

3. Roast in the oven for 25–30 minutes.

4. Cook the pasta (see page 23) 15 minutes from the end of the roasting time.

5. Drain the pasta and add the roasted veg, complete with all the juices. Mix and serve.

Khitcherie

Here the split peas and nuts provide the protein, etc. It can be eaten on its own, or as a rice dish with other things. You can vary the amount of curry paste to your taste.

£1.13 /PERSON

3

2

PREP 30 MINS

1/2 mug **split peas**, soaked overnight

2 tablespoons **oil** to fry

1/2 **onion**, chopped

1 clove **garlic**, chopped

1 **fresh chilli**, chopped

1 teaspoon grated fresh **ginger**

11/2 mugs **water**

1/2 mug **raisins**

1 dessertspoon **curry paste**

1 mug basmati **rice**

1/2 mug toasted **cashews**, roughly chopped

1. Put the split peas in a bowl and cover with cold water. Soak overnight.

2. Heat the oil in a saucepan and add the onions, garlic, chilli and ginger. Stir frequently and cook for 2–3 minutes.

3. Add the rice, drained split peas, water, raisins and curry paste. Bring to the boil, then turn down to simmer for 15 minutes, or until the rice is cooked. The liquid should have almost boiled away. If not, allow to cook a little more. The mixture should not be very dry. If it is, add a little more water. Take off the heat and stir in the toasted cashews.

4. Serve with yogurt.

Bubble and Squeak

If you have any leftover veggies, they are ideal to use in this dish.

£1.09 /PERSON

2

2

PREP 30 MINS

1 small **carrot**, chopped

1 medium **potato**, diced

1 small **sweet potato**, peeled and cut into chunks

1/2 mug frozen **peas**

1 mug shredded **cabbage**

1 tablespoon **oil** to fry

1 small **onion**, chopped

1 dessertspoon **chives**

1/2 mug **toasted cashews**, roughly chopped

1/2 mug grated **cheese**

salt and **pepper**

Tomato Sauce (see page 33)

1. Boil the carrots for 5 minutes in a saucepan, then add the potatoes and sweet potatoes and boil for another 7 minutes. Add the peas and cabbage and boil for a further 3 minutes. Drain the vegetables.

2. Turn the grill on to heat up.

3. Heat a little oil in a frying pan and fry the onions until they begin to brown. Add the drained vegetables and the chives. Fry for 2–3 minutes, stirring frequently. Season well.

4. Sprinkle the top with the grated cheese and the cashews. Place the frying pan under the grill until the cheese is browned.

5. Serve with the Tomato Sauce.

something mum might cook **91**

No Pastry Quiche

You can add other vegetables to the basic recipe at the end of stage 2. Broccoli, squash, etc. will need to be precooked. Eat any leftovers, cold, the next day.

1 tablespoon **oil** to fry

1 **red onion**, cut into wedges

1 **courgette**, cut into chunks

1 **pepper**, cut into chunks

4–5 **cherry tomatoes**, cut in half

4 **eggs**, beaten

1/2 mug **milk**

3/4 mug grated **Parmesan-style cheese**

1 dessertspoon **basil**

salt and **pepper**

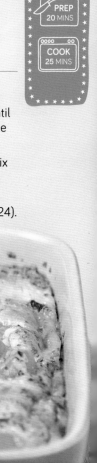

£1.33 /PERSON

2

2

PREP 20 MINS

COOK 25 MINS

1. Preheat the oven to 180°C fan oven/200°C/Gas 6.

2. Fry the onion, pepper and courgette in the oil for 3–4 minutes until they begin to brown. Transfer to a greased casserole dish. Add the tomatoes.

3. Beat the eggs in a bowl and add the milk, Parmesan and basil. Mix well. Season and pour over the vegetables. Cook in the oven for 20-25 minutes until the top begins to brown.

4. Serve either hot or cold, with salad or baked potatoes (see page 24).

Sweet Potato Patties

The yogurt dressing works well with the sweet potatoes, but you can choose other dressings from page 36 and serve with some of the salad recipes.

£0.92 /PERSON

3

2

PREP 15 MINS

COOK 25 MINS

2 medium **sweet potatoes**, peeled and cut into chunks

1 tablespoon **oil** to fry

1 **leek**, chopped

1 clove **garlic**, chopped

1 teaspoon freshly grated **ginger**

salt and **pepper**

2 tablespoons **sweetcorn**, drained

1 tablespoon **fromage frais**

yogurt dressing (page 37)

salad

1. Preheat the oven to 180°C fan oven/200°C/Gas 6.

2. Put the sweet potatoes in boiling water and simmer for 10 minutes.

3. Heat a little oil in a frying pan and fry the leeks, garlic and ginger for 2–3 minutes.

4. Add the sweetcorn. Take off the heat.

5. When the potatoes are cooked, mash them with a fork. Mix in with the rest of the ingredients and season with salt and pepper.

6. Grease a baking tray and spoon the mixture into 4 or 5 piles. Brush the top with a little oil. Cook in the oven for 25 minutes until they are a little brown on the top.

7. Serve with the yogurt dressing and some salad.

something mum might cook **93**

Nutty Crumble

You can vary the vegetables as you wish. If you use broccoli or other vegetables that cook quickly, add towards the end of stage 2.

1 tablespoon **oil** to fry

1 **sweet potato** (you may use normal ones), peeled and chopped

1 **parsnip**, peeled and roughly chopped

1 **carrot**, peeled and chopped

1 **onion**, cut into wedges

1 mug **frozen peas**

400g tin **chopped tomatoes**

1/2 mug **water** + 1 vegetable **stock cube**

Crumble topping

3/4 mug **plain flour**, or equal proportions of buckwheat and plain flour

1/5 x 250g block **butter**

1/2 mug grated **Cheddar cheese**

1/2 mug **nuts**, chopped (use any variety; pine nuts, or cashews work well)

£1.53 /PERSON

3

2-3

PREP 20 MINS

COOK 30 MINS

---

1. Preheat the oven to 170°C fan oven/190°C/Gas 5.

2. Heat the oil in a saucepan and fry the vegetables for 4–5 minutes. Stir frequently. Allow them to brown a little.

3. Add the frozen peas, tomatoes, water and crumbled vegetable stock cube and bring to the boil. Turn down the heat and simmer for 10 minutes, or until they are tender.

4. While the vegetables are cooking, put the flour and butter in a bowl and rub in the butter using your finger ends and thumbs. The mixture should resemble breadcrumbs. Add the cheese and nuts. Mix together.

5. When the vegetables are cooked, pour into a casserole dish. Sprinkle the crumble mixture, evenly, over the top. Press down gently to compact the crumble.

6. Cook in the oven for 25-30 minutes.

Nut and Tomato Roast

OK to eat hot or cold, so will be ideal for lunch the next day. You can use the tomato sauce with other dishes too.

£1.80 /PERSON

3

2

PREP
20 MINS

COOK
25 MINS

1 large **potato**, diced

1 tablespoon **oil** to fry

1 small **onion**, chopped

1 clove **garlic**, chopped

3 medium **mushrooms**, chopped

4 pieces of **sun-dried tomato**, chopped

100g packet of mixed **nuts**, chopped

1 slice granary or **wholemeal bread**, made into crumbs

1/4 mug water + 1 vegetable **stock cube**, crumbled

1/2 teaspoon **chives** or **coriander**

1 **egg**

salt and **pepper**

Tomato sauce

3 tablespoons **crème fraîche**

1 teaspoon **tomato purée**

1 teaspoon **honey**

1/2 teaspoon **coriander** or **basil**

1 teaspoon **chives**

1. Preheat the oven to 180°C fan oven/200°C/Gas 6. Grease a loaf tin. Put a piece of greaseproof paper in the bottom.

2. Put the potato in boiling water and simmer for 10 minutes until it is cooked. Drain and mash a little with a fork.

3. Heat the oil in a frying pan and cook the onion and garlic for 3–4 minutes. Add the mushrooms and sun-dried tomatoes. Set to one side.

4. In a bowl, mix together the potatoes, nuts, breadcrumbs, stock, water, chives and egg. Season with salt and pepper.

5. Spread half the potato and nut mixture evenly into the bottom of the loaf tin. Place the tomato mix over the top and spread evenly. Add the rest of the potato mixture to make the top layer. Cook for 25 minutes in the oven. Leave to cool a little, before trying to get the roast out of the tin.

6. To make the tomato sauce, simply mix all the ingredients together.

Corn Cakes & Ratatouille

These are best eaten straight away. You can keep the batter for making the corn cakes in the fridge for the next day, but no longer. Ratatouille is a versatile dish and goes well with bean burgers, vegetarian sausages, or any of the patty recipes in this book.

£1.46 /PERSON

3

2

PREP 25 MINS

Ratatouille

1 tablespoon **oil** to fry

1/2 **onion**, chopped

1 small clove **garlic**, chopped

1 **baby aubergine**, sliced

1 small **courgette**, sliced

1 **red** or **green pepper**, sliced

2 large **mushrooms**, sliced

400g tin **chopped tomatoes**

salt and **pepper**

Corn Cakes

2/3 mug **self-raising flour**

1 **egg**

1/3 mug **milk**

130g can of **sweetcorn**, drained

1 tablespoon **oil** to fry

1. To make the ratatouille, heat the oil in a saucepan. Add the onions and garlic and cook for 3–4 minutes until the onions begin to brown. Add the other vegetables and allow them to fry a little. When they are beginning to cook, add the tin of tomatoes. Season. Bring to the boil and then turn down to simmer for 10 minutes.

2. To make the corn cakes, put the flour in a bowl (you can use half ordinary flour and half buckwheat flour if you wish). Make a well in the centre and add the egg and some of the milk. Beat with a wooden spoon. Add enough milk to make a thick, creamy consistency. Add the drained corn. This will make the batter thinner.

3. Heat the oil in a frying pan. Drop 3 or 4 separate heaped tablespoons of the batter mixture into the pan. Allow them to cook and become solid and browned underneath. Turn them over and allow them to brown on the other side. They should be cooked in the middle. If not, turn down the heat and cook for a little longer.

4. Serve with the ratatouille.

Veggie Bake with Tomato Sauce

Veggie bake is another easy, basic recipe, which can be varied by using different vegetables and also different sauces. You can use the Tomato Sauce or Quick Cheese Sauce recipes on page 33. Always put the grated cheese on the top, to give a tasty crunch.

£1.27 /PERSON

2

2

PREP 20 MINS

COOK 30 MINS

1 **carrot**, diced

1 **potato**, diced

1 medium **sweet potato**, peeled and cut into chunks

4–5 **spring onions** or 1 small onion, chopped

1 tablespoon **oil** to fry

1 **courgette**, sliced

3–4 **cherry tomatoes**

1 teaspoon **chives**

1/2 mug grated **cheese**

Tomato Sauce (see page 33)

1. Boil the carrots, potatoes, sweet potatoes and any other root vegetables you are using for 10 minutes.

2. Preheat the oven to 180°C fan oven/200°C/Gas 6.

3. Fry the onions and courgettes. Once they begin to brown, take off the heat.

4. Drain the root vegetables and return them to the pan. Add the onions and courgettes, together with the tomatoes, chives and tomato sauce. Mix together and then pour into a greased casserole dish. Top with grated cheese. Bake in the oven for 25-30 minutes until the cheese is browned.

Honey Mushroom and Rice Pie

Ready-rolled pastry is really handy and easy to use. It adds a little more variety to your food.

1 mug **water**

1/2 mug **rice**

1 teaspoon **pilau rice seasoning**

1 tablespoon **oil** to fry

2 **onions**, sliced

100g pack **pine nuts**

250g pack **mushrooms**, sliced

2 teaspoons **fennel seeds**

2 teaspoons **honey**

375g pack ready-rolled **puff pastry**

1 beaten **egg**

salt and **pepper**

£2.11 /PERSON

4

3-4

PREP 25 MINS

COOK 25 MINS

1. Preheat the oven to 200°C fan oven/220°C/Gas 7.

2. Put the mug of water on to boil. Add the rice and pilau rice seasoning and bring back to the boil. Turn down to simmer for 10–15 minutes.

3. Heat the oil in a pan and fry the onions until they become soft. Add the pine nuts and fry until they become slightly brown. Add the mushrooms and fry for 30 seconds. Add the fennel seeds and the honey. Season with salt and pepper.

4. Put half the onion and mushrooms on the bottom of a small casserole dish. Put the rice on top, with the rest of the onions and mushrooms on top of the rice.

5. Unroll the pastry and place on top of the pie. Cut to size and pinch the edges. Brush the top with beaten egg.

6. Place in the oven for 20–25 minutes until browned on top.

Carrot Pancakes, Houmous and Salad

The houmous will keep until the next day and is great eaten with some celery sticks.

£1.25 /PERSON

3

2-3

PREP 30 MINS

Houmous

400g tin **chickpeas**, rinsed and drained

4 **sun-dried tomatoes**, chopped

juice of a **lemon**

1 tablespoon **olive oil**

Pancakes

2 **eggs**

1/2 mug **self-raising flour**

1 teaspoon ground **cumin**

1 teaspoon ground **coriander**

1 small **onion**, grated

3 **carrots**, peeled and grated

oil to fry

Salad

1 little gem **lettuce**, cut horizontally

2 **spring onions**, cut into thin strips

7cm piece of **cucumber**, cut into strips

1 green eating **apple**, cut into thin wedges

Dressing – chose from page 36

1. Make the salad dressing. Set to one side until needed.

2. Mix together the houmous ingredients and blitz with a hand-held blender. Season with salt and pepper.

3. Beat the eggs in a bowl and add the flour, cumin and coriander. Beat together. Season well with salt and pepper.

4. Squeeze the excess water from the grated onions and carrots. Add to the egg mixture and mix well.

5. Heat a little oil in a frying pan and add the pancake mix, 1 tablespoon at a time. Fry on each side for 1–2 minutes on a medium heat. Repeat until the pancake mix is used up.

6. Serve the houmous with the pancakes and salad.

Roast Vegetables, Mash and Tomato Sauce

£1.52 /PERSON

You could just use tomato sauce, but, if you make the one below, you will have some left for another day.

Roast Veg

1 **courgette**, cut into 1cm pieces

1 small **aubergine**, cut into 1cm slices

1 **red pepper**, cut into chunks

1 **red onion**, cut into wedges

1 **sweet potato**, peeled and cut into chunks

2 tablespoons **oil**

salt and **pepper**

Mash

1 large **potato**, peeled and cut into 4cm cubes

400g tin **haricot beans**, washed and drained

salt and **pepper**

2 x 2cm cube **butter**

Piquant Tomato Sauce
(see page 32)

1. Preheat the oven to 200°C fan oven/220°C/Gas 7.

2. Put the vegetables for roasting on a baking tray. Drizzle with the oil and season well. Use your hands to distribute the oil and seasoning evenly. Place in the oven for 25–30 minutes   until browned.

3. Put the potatoes in boiling water, bring to the boil, then turn down to simmer for 10 minutes. Add the beans in a pan, bring to the boil, simmer for 2 minutes. Drain.

4. Mash together with the butter. Serve with the roast veg and tomato sauce.

something for the weekend

Got a little more time on your hands and fancy something a bit different to eat? Treat yourself to something from this section.

something for the weekend

Korma Beans with Naan

A spicy twist on the traditional beans on toast. If you like your food really spicy, try different curry pastes.

£1.44 /PERSON

2

2

PREP 15 MINS

1 tablespoon **oil** to fry

1 medium **onion**, cut into thin wedges

1/2 **green pepper**, cut into thin slices

1 tablespoon **Korma curry paste**

4 medium **tomatoes**, cut into chunks

400g **cannellini beans**, rinsed and drained

1 tablespoon chopped, **fresh coriander**

2 **peshwari naan breads**

yogurt to serve

1. Preheat the oven to 200°C fan oven/220°C/Gas 7.

2. Heat the oil in a frying pan, add the onions and peppers and fry for 2–3 minutes or until they are golden brown.

3. Put the naan bread in the preheated oven for 3 minutes (need to verify this timing on the packet).

4. Add the curry paste and cook on medium heat for 30 seconds, stir frequently.

5. Add the tomatoes and beans and cook for a further 1 minute, stirring frequently. Add the coriander.

6. Take the naan bread out of the oven.

7. Add the drained beans and coriander to the frying pan and cook for 1 minute, stirring frequently.

8. Serve with the naan breads and a tablespoon of yogurt.

Spaghetti Bolognese

If you want to vary this recipe, you can add half a teaspoon of Marmite or HP sauce at stage 2.

£0.79 /PERSON

2

2

PREP 30 MINS

1 small **onion**, chopped

1 small **carrot**, finely chopped

1 **celery stick**, chopped

1/2 **red pepper**, chopped

1 tablespoon **oil** to fry

2 tablespoons **red lentils**

400g can **chopped tomatoes**

1 teaspoon **oregano**

1 mug **water** + 1 vegetable **stock cube**, crumbled

2 portions of **spaghetti** to serve (see page 23)

grated **Parmesan-style** or **Cheddar cheese** to serve

1. Finely chop all the vegetables and fry with the oil in a saucepan for 3–4 minutes.

2. Add the lentils, tomatoes, oregano, stock cube and water. Bring to the boil. Season with salt and pepper. Leave to simmer for about 20 minutes until all the vegetables are cooked.

3. In the meantime, put the spaghetti on to cook (see page 23).

4. When everything is cooked, drain the spaghetti and serve the bolognese mixture on the top. Grate some Parmesan-style or Cheddar cheese over the top.

Pasta and Pepper Sauce

This is a good snack meal. You could add a few fried vegetables, such as mushrooms or courgettes if you wish.

£0.76 /PERSON

2

2

PREP 30 MINS

1 **red pepper**, deseeded and cut in half

2 **tomatoes**, chopped into pieces

1 **clove garlic**, whole

1 **red chilli**, deseeded and cut in half

2 tablespoons **oil**

1 teaspoon **oregano**

2 portions of **pasta** (see page 23)

1. Preheat the oven to 180°C fan oven/200°C/Gas 6. Place the peppers, chilli, tomatoes and garlic on a baking sheet and brush with the oil. Roast for 20 minutes.

2. Put the pasta on to cook (see page 23).

3. Once roasted, put the peppers, tomatoes, chilli, garlic and oregano in a bowl and whizz with the hand-held blender. Warm the sauce through again.

4. When the pasta is cooked, drain and put on plates. Pour the sauce over the top.

5. If you want to add vegetables to this, simply chop them up, fry them in a frying pan and add the sauce and mix together.

Split Pea Risotto

You need to plan in advance for this one, as the split peas need soaking overnight and the cooking time is quite long.

1/3 mug **yellow, split peas**, soaked overnight

1 tablespoon **oil** to fry

1 medium **onion**, chopped

1 **clove garlic**, chopped

1 medium **potato**, diced

2 **tomatoes**, chopped

1/4 mug **long grain rice**

1 mug **water**

1 vegetable **stock cube**

1 dessertspoon **curry paste**

juice of 1/2 **lemon**

1 teaspoon **coriander**

1. Drain the peas and rinse.

2. Heat the oil in a saucepan. Fry the onions, garlic, potato and tomatoes. Cook for 2–3 minutes.

3. Add the rice, water, crumbled stock cube, curry paste and the split peas. Bring to the boil and then turn down to simmer. Cover with a lid and cook for 1 hour. Check every now and then to make sure it is not boiling dry. If it gets dry, add a little more water.

4. Once everything is cooked, add the lemon juice and coriander. Stir. There should not be too much liquid left. If so, simmer for about 5 minutes, without the lid on the pan, to reduce the liquid.

Sweet and Spicy Pilau

This is an appetizing rice salad, full of good things. Good to eat on its own as a snack, or with some green salad.

1 tablespoon **oil** to fry

1 **onion**, sliced

1/2 mug **basmati rice**

1 1/2 mugs **water**

1/2 teaspoon **chilli powder**

1/4 mug **currants**

1/4 mug **ready-to-eat apricots**, chopped

1/4 mug **sultanas**, currants, or raisins

1/4 mug **pine nuts** or almonds

£1.26 /PERSON

2

2

PREP 30 MINS

1. Heat the oil in a saucepan and fry the onions until they become caramelised (go quite brown).

2. Add the rice, water and chilli powder. Bring to the boil, then turn down to simmer for about 10–15 minutes, uncovered until the rice is cooked and the water has been absorbed.

3. Take off the heat and stir in the fruit and nuts. Leave to stand.

Spinach, Bean and Potato Bake

Take care not to overcook the spinach, as it really just needs to wilt a little.

£1.70 /PERSON

3

3-4

PREP 20 MINS

COOK 20 MINS

1 medium **potato**, cut into bite-sized pieces

1 medium **sweet potato**, cut into bite-sized pieces

2cm cube **butter**

1 tablespoon **oil** to fry

200g pack fresh **spinach**

1 **onion**, sliced

100g pack **pine nuts**

2 teaspoons **cumin seeds**

2 teaspoons **honey**

400g tin **cannellini beans**, washed and drained

1. Preheat the oven to 180°C fan oven/200°C/Gas 6.

2. Put the potatoes and sweet potatoes on to simmer for 10 minutes. Drain, return to the pan and add the butter. Shake around to distribute evenly.

3. Heat a little oil in a wok and add the spinach. Fry for 1/2–1 minute until the spinach is wilted but not mushy. Tip into the bottom of a casserole dish.

4. Heat a little oil in the wok and add the onions and pine nuts. Fry until they brown a little.

5. Add the fennel seeds, honey and drained beans. Mix together and then place on top of the spinach in the casserole dish.

6. Put the potato mix on top. Place in the oven for 20 minutes until the top is slightly browned.

Potato and Nut Terrine

Serve with baked potatoes, salads, or one of the sauces on pages 32 and 33. You can eat it hot or cold, so it's OK to have for lunches and snacks the next day. It is served here with Apple and Bean salad (see page 60).

£1.62 /PERSON

3

4

PREP 25 MINS

COOK 55 MINS

2 medium **potatoes**, diced

1 **red onion**, chopped

2 **cloves garlic**, chopped

4-5 **mushrooms**, chopped

1 tablespoon **oil** to fry

1 tablespoon **curry paste**

4 **eggs**, beaten

1/2 x 250g pack of **cream cheese**, softened

200g pack of **pecan nuts**, roughly chopped

200g pack of **cashew nuts**, roughly chopped

1/2 mug grated **Parmesan-style cheese**

serve with a **sauce**, or **salad**

1. Preheat the oven to 170°C fan oven/190°C/Gas 5. Grease a loaf tin and put a piece of greaseproof paper across the bottom.

2. Cook the potatoes in boiling water for 10 minutes. Drain and mash slightly with a fork. It does not need to be smooth.

3. Fry the onions, garlic and mushrooms in the oil for 4-5 minutes until they are softened. Add the curry paste and stir well. Add this to the potatoes in the saucepan, along with the eggs, cream cheese, nuts and Parmesan. Season well and mix together.

4. Put the mixture into the loaf tin and bake in the oven for 45 minutes. Serve, hot or cold, with a sauce or salad.

If you like your loaf nutty, check out this fennel and chestnut loaf! noshbooks.com/nutty-loaf

Nut and Courgette Slice

The slice is served here with salad and a yogurt dressing (page 37).

1 tablespoon **oil** to fry

1 small **onion**, chopped

1 **clove garlic**, chopped

2 **eggs**, beaten

2 tablespoons **milk**

1 slice **bread** made into breadcrumbs

1 large **courgette**, grated

1 small **carrot**, grated

200g pack mixed **chopped nuts**

1/2 mug grated **Cheddar cheese**

salt and **pepper**

£1.79 /PERSON

2

2

PREP 15 MINS

COOK 40 MINS

1. Preheat the oven to 180°C fan oven/200°C/Gas 6. Grease a loaf tin and put a piece of greaseproof paper on the bottom.

2. Heat a little oil in a frying pan and fry the onion and garlic in a saucepan for 2–3 minutes.

3. Take off the heat. Add the rest of the ingredients and mix well.

4. Pour into the loaf tin and press down evenly. Bake in the oven for 35–40 minutes until browned on top.

5. Make sure the sides are loosened from the loaf tin and tip out. Once cooled, serve sliced with salad and a dressing.

Mediterranean Bulgar Wheat Salad

Use up any leftover feta in sandwiches. Great with tomatoes.

£1.37 /PERSON

1

2-3

PREP 30 MINS

1/2 mug **bulgar wheat**

1 vegetable **stock cube** + 3/4 mug boiling **water** for bulgar wheat

6 **cherry tomatoes**, each cut in 1/2

3 **spring onions**, chopped

1 medium **avocado**, peeled and cut into wedges

12 **olives**, halved

1/2 x 200g pack **feta**, cut into small cubes

1/2 **red pepper**, sliced thinly

green salad

Dressing

1 tablespoon **olive oil**

juice of 1/2 **lemon**

1 teaspoon **sugar**

1 dessertspoon chopped **fresh basil**

salt and **pepper**

1. Put the water and stock cube on to boil. Once boiling, add the bulgar wheat and simmer for 5 minutes. The liquid should be absorbed. Allow to cool.

2. Mix the dressing ingredients together and set aside until needed.

3. Arrange the green salad on individual plates.

4. Mix the tomatoes, olives, spring onions and pepper into the cooled bulgar wheat. Arrange over the salad.

5. Place the avocado and feta cheese over the bulgar wheat and drizzle the dressing over.

117

Chickpea Frittata

Frittata is basically an omelette with loads of stuff in it. This gives some idea of how to make it. You can vary the things you put in; different varieties of beans would work well in this recipe.

1 tablespoon **oil** to fry

1/2 **onion**, finely chopped

1 small **clove garlic**, chopped

400g can of **chickpeas**, well rinsed and drained

1 large **tomato**, chopped

1 teaspoon **oregano**

1 tablespoon **chives**

4 **eggs**, beaten

1/2 mug grated **cheese**

Salsa

1 medium **avocado**, chopped

1 small **red onion**, thinly sliced

2 **tomatoes**, chopped

1/2 teaspoon **chilli powder**

2 tablespoons **olive oil**

juice of 1/2 **lemon**

1 teaspoon **sugar**

1. To make up the salsa, mix the ingredients together and leave to stand while you make the frittata. See page 147 for different salsas.

2. Fry the onion and garlic in a frying pan. Cook until the onion is soft.

3. Turn the grill on to heat up.

4. Add the chickpeas and tomato to the frying pan and mix. Add the herbs to the beaten eggs and pour into the frying pan over the bean mixture. Don't stir the frittata. Cook on a medium heat for about 5 minutes until the egg begins to set. It does not need to be completely set. Sprinkle the grated cheese over the top of the frittata and place under a hot grill for about 5 minutes until the cheese is browned and the eggs are set.

5. Serve with the salsa or one of the sauces on pages 32 and 33.

For another frittata idea, check out Joy's Sweet Potato and Spinach Fritatta
noshbooks.com/spinach

Goat's Cheese Tart with Black Olives

You can use the base of this tart almost like a pizza. Add a Tomato sauce (see pages 32 & 33), plus some vegetables and cheese and invent your own pizzas.

£1.58 /PERSON

3

2

PREP 15 MINS

COOK 25 MINS

Base

1 tablespoon **oil** to fry

¹/₂ an **onion**, finely chopped

1 mug **self-raising flour**

50g or ¹/₅ x 250g block **butter**

1 **egg**, beaten

Topping

8 **cherry tomatoes**

15-18 **black olives**

125g packet of **soft goat's cheese**

1. Heat a little oil in a frying pan and fry the onion until it begins to brown. Set aside.

2. Preheat the oven to 180°C fan oven/200°C/Gas 6.

3. Put the flour in a bowl and rub in the butter. Add the onions and the beaten egg. If the mixture is still dry, add a little more milk.

4. Tip out onto a surface and squash together. Place on a greased baking tray and squash out gently with your fingers to make a round. It should be about 1.5cm thick.

5. Cut the tomatoes in half and spread over the top with the olives and the crumbled cheese. Drizzle oil over the top.

6. Bake in the oven for 25 minutes. Serve with salad and sprinkle some French dressing (see page 36), or olive oil, over the tart.

Lentil and Tofu Bake

You could exchange the tofu for cubed Quorn if you wish, see pt. 5.

£1.91 /PERSON

2

2

PREP 30 MINS

COOK 30 MINS

3 medium **potatoes**, diced

3–4 **broccoli florets**

2cm cube butter for the **potatoes**

1/2 mug **red lentils**

1 tablespoon **oil** to fry

1 **leek**, sliced

1 **clove garlic**, chopped

1 **celery** stick, chopped

2 teaspoons **tomato purée**

1/2 x 100g pack **pine nuts**

1/2 x 350g pack **tofu**, cut into cubes

1/2 mug grated **cheese**

salt and **pepper**

1. Preheat the oven to 180°C fan oven/200°C/Gas 6.

2. Put the potatoes in boiling water, simmer for the 5 minutes, then add the broccoli and simmer for a further 5 minutes. Drain. Take the broccoli out and set aside. Add some butter to the potatoes and shake them in the pan. Set to one side.

3. Simmer the lentils for 15-20 minutes until they are tender, then drain.

4. Heat a little oil in a frying pan and fry the leeks, garlic and celery for 3–4 minutes until they begin to brown.

5. Add the tomato purée, lentils, pine nuts, tofu (or Quorn) and the broccoli. Mix well, season with salt and pepper, then pour into a greased casserole dish. Put the potatoes on the top and sprinkle with the grated cheese.

6. Bake in the oven for 25-30 minutes until the cheese is browned.

7. Serve with a tomato sauce (page 32 & 33).

Chilli Courgette Torte

Eat it on its own, with green salad, or one of the other salads in this book.

£1.16 /PERSON

1 tablespoon **oil** to fry

2 medium **courgettes**, sliced

1 small **onion**, chopped

1 fresh **green chilli**, chopped

2 **eggs**

1/2 teaspoon **paprika**

1/2 mug grated **Cheddar cheese**

PREP 15 MINS

COOK 25 MINS

1. Preheat the oven to 170°C fan oven/190°C/Gas 5. Grease a casserole dish.

2. Heat the oil in a frying pan and fry the courgettes. Transfer to a casserole dish.

3. Fry the onion and the chilli until they begin to brown. Add to the casserole dish.

4. Beat the eggs, then add the paprika to them. Pour the egg mixture over the courgettes. Sprinkle the cheese over the top. Bake in the oven for 25-30 minutes until the cheese has browned and the eggs are set.

Savoury Pancakes

Savoury pancakes are made in exactly the same way as sweet ones. Add savoury fillings and they can turn from fun food to a serious meal.

2 **eggs**

6 tablespoons **self-raising flour** (you can use one half bulgar wheat flour and one half self-raising flour)

milk

Trex or white Flora to fry (you can use oil but a lard type is best)

Suggested fillings

You can use any of the fillings for fajitas (pages 144 &145).

Use some of the different sauces (pages 32 & 33). Quick Cheese Sauce has been used in the photo.

1. Beat the eggs and flour together in a bowl or jug. Gradually add the milk whilst mixing, making sure there are no lumps. The mixture should be as thin as single cream, quite thin, but not as thin as milk.

2. Heat about 1.5cm cube of lard in a frying pan. When the fat begins to smoke a little, pour approximately 2 tablespoons of the mixture into the pan. Tip the pan around so that the mixture spreads over the surface of the pan. Let the mixture cook for about 1 minute.

3. Gently lift the edge of the pancake to see if it is browned. Once browned, turn the pancake with a slotted turner, or toss and then cook the other side. Serving suggestions above.

Tofu Balls with Tomato Sauce

A good recipe to make tofu a bit more tasty. The Tomato sauce is essential.
Serve with rice.

£1.15 /PERSON

2

2

PREP
15 MINS

COOK
30 MINS

Tofu balls

1 small **onion**, finely chopped

1 small **garlic clove**, finely chopped

1/2 x 375g pack **tofu**, chopped

1/4 mug **breadcrumbs**

1 tablespoon **flour**

1 tablespoon **soy sauce**

1 teaspoon **dried chives**

1 teaspoon **dried basil**

salt and **pepper**

Tomato sauce

1 tablespoon **oil** to fry

1 **clove garlic**, finely chopped

1 medium **onion**, chopped

400g can **chopped tomatoes**

1 tablespoon **tomato purée**

salt and **pepper**

rice to serve (see page 22)

1. Preheat the oven to 180°C fan oven/200°C/Gas 6.

2. Put all the tofu balls ingredients together in a bowl and mix well. Form into balls and place on a greased baking tray. Cook in the oven for 25-30 minutes until they are browned.

3. While they are cooking, put the rice on to cook (see page 22).

4. To make the sauce, fry the onions and garlic in a saucepan, add the tomatoes and tomato purée. Cook for about 5 minutes. Season with salt and pepper. Whizz with the blender.

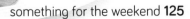

Roast Vegetable with Chunky Tofu

Tofu is high in protein and contains calcium, iron and Vitamins B1, B2 and B3. It is, however, fairly bland in taste and therefore needs to be eaten with other, more tasty, foods.

£1.80 /PERSON

1

1

PREP 10 MINS

COOK 45 MINS

1/2 x 350g block of **tofu**

1/2 **onion** cut into wedges

1 small **sweet potato**, peeled and cut into small chunks

1 small **courgette**, cut into small chunks

1/2 **red pepper**, chopped

1 teaspoon **rosemary** (optional)

1 tablespoon **oil**

salt and **pepper**

1. Preheat the oven to 200°C fan oven/220°C/Gas 7.

2. Cut the tofu up into chunks.

3. Place all the ingredients into a casserole dish, sprinkle olive oil over and mix to cover all the ingredients in oil.

4. Season with salt and pepper and sprinkle with rosemary if you have some. Bake in the oven for 45 minutes until nicely browned.

Red Chilli Tofu

This won't reheat well, so best shared with a friend.

£1.69 /PERSON

2

2

PREP 25 MINS

1 tablespoon **oil** to fry

1 **onion**, chopped

1 **clove garlic**, chopped

349g pack firm **soya bean curd** or **tofu**, cubed

1 fat **red chilli**, chopped

2 tablespoons **soy sauce**

1 tablespoon **white wine vinegar**

1 teaspoon **sugar** or honey

300g tin **broad beans**, drained. Try to get frozen soy beans

1 teaspoon **dried coriander**

rice to serve (see page 22)

1. Put the rice on to cook (see page 22).
2. Heat the oil in a wok and add the onions, garlic and the tofu, Fry until browned.
3. Add the chilli and fry for 30 seconds.
4. Add the rest of the ingredients and cook for 2 minutes, on a high heat, stirring frequently.
5. Serve with rice.

friends around

Want to impress your friends, but not sure how? Here is something for when there is a hungry crowd to feed.

friends around

Fried Halloumi Salad with Pine Nut Couscous

Bags of green salad are very convenient. A cheaper way is to buy a small lettuce, some cucumber and spring onions. This will make a larger quantity for about the same price.

£2.32 /PERSON

1

2-3

PREP 25 MINS

1/2 mug **couscous**

1/2 vegetable **stock cube** + 1 mug boiling **water**

4 **spring onions**, chopped

1 **red apple**, chopped

1/2 x 100g pack of **pine nuts**

2 sticks **celery**, chopped

1 tablespoon **oil** to fry

250g pack of **halloumi cheese**, sliced

Dressing

2 tablespoons **olive oil**

juice of a **lemon**

2 tablespoons chopped fresh **mint**

1 teaspoon **sugar**

salt and **pepper**

green salad

1. Put the couscous in a bowl and pour over the boiling stock. Cover and leave for 4–5 minutes.

2. Once cooled, add the onions, apple, celery and pine nuts.

3. Mix the dressing ingredients together and set to one side until needed.

4. Heat the oil in a frying pan and fry the halloumi on a fairly high heat until it becomes a little browned.

5. Arrange the green salad on the individual plates. Put the couscous mix over the top and place the halloumi on top of that. Drizzle over the rest of the dressing.

Mango and Noodle Salad

This is best served hot, since it does not reheat well. You can use the leftover mango from this recipe in a smoothie.

£1.24 /PERSON

2

2

PREP 15 MINS

1/2 ripe **mango**

1 tablespoon **oil** to fry

3 **spring onions**, chopped

2 cloves **garlic**, chopped

1/2 **red pepper**, sliced

1/2 **yellow pepper**, sliced

1/2 **red chilli**, deseeded and chopped

1/2 x 200g pack of ready-to-eat free-range **eggless noodles**

Dressing

2 tablespoons peanut butter

1/3 mug coconut milk

1/2 teaspoon tomato purée

1. Peel the mango and slice off the main sections, cutting around the stone. Cut into strips.

2. To make the dressing, just mix the ingredients together until smooth.

3. Heat the oil in a frying pan. Fry the onions, garlic, peppers and chilli for 4–5 minutes. The onions should be softened.

4. Add the mango and the noodles. Cook for 3–4 minutes, stirring frequently. Once everything is heated through, transfer to serving plates and pour the peanut sauce over the top.

Nut and Carrot Coleslaw

You can eat this with other salads or with baked potatoes and cheese. It is so much better than coleslaw you might buy, ready-made, from a supermarket. If you want to keep half for the next day, divide in 2 before you put the dressing on.

£0.60 /PERSON

1

2

PREP 15 MINS

3 tablespoons **olive oil**

1 tablespoon **chives**

2 tablespoons **white wine vinegar**

1 teaspoon **sugar**

salt and **pepper**

1 **carrot**, grated

3 **spring onions**, cut into long strips

2 **celery** sticks, chopped

1/8 small hard **white cabbage** (you could use Chinese cabbage if you wish)

1/2 mug **cashew nuts**

1. Mix together the oil, chives, wine vinegar, sugar and salt and pepper.

2. Put all the other ingredients in a bowl and mix with a spoon. Pour the dressing over and mix.

For more cakes and cookies go to noshbooks.com/salads

Fruit'n Nut Salad

This salad has lots of healthy things in it. It has a yummy, crunchy, sweet-and-savoury flavour. You can eat it as a snack by itself, or to accompany vegetarian sausages or bean burgers.

3/4 mug basmati **rice**, cooked in 1 1/2 mugs water with 1 teaspoon **pilau rice seasoning**

1 tablespoon **oil** to fry

1 medium **onion**, chopped

1 tablespoon **turmeric**

1 teaspoon **curry paste**

grated rind of 1 **lemon**

1/2 mug **pine nuts**

1/2 mug **dates**, chopped

1/2 mug ready-to-eat **figs**, chopped

2 sticks **celery**, chopped

4 heaped tablespoons **mayonnaise**

juice of a **lemon**

1/2 mug **pecan nuts**, roughly chopped

1. Cook the rice with the pilau rice seasoning (see page 22).

2. Fry the onions until they begin to brown. Add the turmeric and curry paste and mix well. Cook for 2–3 minutes. Add the rest of the ingredients and mix.

Spanish Baked Eggs

Best cooked for 2 and shared, since the eggs won't reheat too well. You can eat it cold with some salad. You could also eat it with some vegetarian sausages.

£0.97 /PERSON

2

2

PREP 15 MINS

COOK 15 MINS

2 large **potatoes**, washed and diced

1 tablespoon **oil** to fry

1 small **onion**, cut into wedges

1 clove **garlic**, chopped

1/2 **green pepper**, chopped

400g can **chopped tomatoes**

1/2 teaspoon **paprika**

1 teaspoon **dried chives**

18 pitted **black olives**

4 **eggs**

salt and **pepper**

1. Preheat the oven to 200°C fan oven/220°C/Gas 7.

2. Cook the diced potatoes in boiling water for about 10 minutes. Drain.

3. Heat the oil in a frying pan and cook the onion, garlic and peppers for 2-3 minutes. Add the tomatoes, paprika, chives and olives. Cook for 2 minutes. Add the potatoes and mix well.

4. Place in a greased casserole dish. Make 4 hollows in the mixture and break an egg into each. Season with salt and pepper.

5. Bake in the oven for 15 minutes, or until the eggs are cooked.

Vegetable Lasagna

Lasagna is good for feeding large numbers of people. Just multiply these ingredients accordingly. You can obviously vary the vegetables you use. Any root vegetables will need to be precooked.

1 tablespoon **oil** to fry

1 small **onion**, chopped

1 clove **garlic**, chopped

1/2 **red pepper**, sliced

4 **mushrooms**, sliced

2 sticks **celery**, sliced

1 small **aubergine**, cut into chunks

1 small **courgette**, sliced

400g tin **chopped tomatoes**

1 teaspoon **mixed herbs**

2 x quantity of **Quick Cheese Sauce** (see page 33)

6 **lasagna sheets**

1/2 mug grated **Cheddar cheese**

1. Preheat the oven to 180°C fan oven/200°C/Gas 6.

2. Heat the oil in a wok and fry the onion, garlic, peppers, mushroom, celery, aubergine and courgette for 4–5 minutes. Add the tin of tomatoes and the herbs and bring to the boil. Simmer for 5 minutes.

3. Make the double quantity of Quick Cheese Sauce (see page 33).

4. Put half the vegetable mixture in the bottom of a casserole dish. Cover with one layer of lasagna strips. Pour half the cheese sauce over. Cover with another layer of lasagna strips. Put the rest of the vegetables on top. Cover with another layer of lasagna strips. Pour over the rest of the cheese sauce. Top with the grated cheese.

5. Cook in the oven for 25-30 minutes. Test the pasta to see if it is cooked. If it has not, turn the oven down to 160°C fan oven/180°C/Gas 4 and cook for another 5–10 minutes.

6. Serve with salad.

Chickpea Patties with Yogurt Dressing

Chickpeas are an important source of protein. If you want to use any of the patties for the next day, leave them unfried and keep them covered in the fridge.

£1.15 /PERSON

3

2

PREP 25 MINS

Patties

400g tin of **chickpeas**, rinsed and drained

1/2 **onion**, grated

1 small **courgette**, grated

1 slice of wholemeal **bread**, made into breadcrumbs

1 **egg**, beaten

1 teaspoon dried **chives**

1 tablespoon **oil** to fry

Yogurt dressing

3 tablespoons **natural yogurt**

1 tablespoon **mango** or **fruit chutney**

1 teaspoon **mint**

Spicy onions

1 tablespoon **oil** to fry

1 large **onion**, sliced

1 teaspoon **curry paste**

---

1. Roughly mash the drained chickpeas with a fork.

2. Squeeze the water out of the grated onion. Mix the onion together in a bowl with the grated courgette, chives and chickpeas.

3. Mix the egg and breadcrumbs together in a separate bowl or mug. This helps the bread to soak and mix more easily with the other ingredients. Add to the chickpea mix. The mixture should be fairly stiff. Tip out onto a surface and, with floured hands, form 4 patties.

4. Heat the oil in a frying pan and put the patties in to fry. Keep the heat moderate and cook for about 5 minutes each side.

5. While they are cooking, mix the yogurt sauce ingredients together.

6. To make the spicy onions, fry the sliced onions in a saucepan on a fairly high heat. Allow them to brown, then add the curry paste and mix well. Cook for 1 minute and then take off the heat.

Koftas with Mango Yogurt Dip

These have 4 stars because they are fiddly and take some time to make, not because they are particularly difficult. My family devoured these as soon as the photograph was taken. The yogurt dressing really makes the dish, so don't miss out on it.

£0.68 /PERSON

4

3-4

PREP 30 MINS

COOK 20 MINS

1 tablespoon **oil** to fry

1/2 **onion**, finely chopped

1 clove **garlic**, finely chopped

1 **carrot**, finely chopped

1 **celery** stick, finely chopped

1 **chilli**, deseeded and chopped

1¹/2 mugs **water**

1 vegetable **stock cube**

1 dessertspoon **curry paste**

2/3 mug **red lentils**

1 tablespoon **tomato purée**

1/3 mug **cashews**

1 mug fresh **breadcrumbs**

1 small **egg**, beaten

salt and **pepper**

Yogurt dip

3 tablespoons **natural yogurt**

1 tablespoon **mango chutney**

1 teaspoon **coriander** or oregano

1. Heat the oil in a saucepan. Fry the onions, garlic, carrot, celery and chilli for 2–3 minutes until the onions start to soften.

2. Add the water, crumbled stock cube, curry paste, lentils and tomato purée. Bring to the boil. Turn down to simmer, with the lid on, for 20 minutes. Check every now and then to see that it has not boiled dry and to stir. If, after the 20 minutes, it is still very wet, cook for a further 5 minutes with the lid off. The mixture should be like a paste. Leave to cool.

3. Chop or whizz the cashew nuts, but not too fine. Crumble the breadcrumbs (you could whizz with the blender). Add the bread, egg, coriander, nuts and seasoning to the mixture in the pan. Stir well.

4. Preheat the oven to 160°C fan oven/180°C/Gas 4.

5. Grease a baking tray. Spoon the dessertspoons of the mixture onto the greased baking tray and form them into balls, see photo. It should make about 20. Put in the oven for 15-20 minutes until they are brown.

6. Mix the dip ingredients together and serve with the hot koftas.

Cannelloni

This is dinner party food. It is so fiddly to fill the cannelloni shells, hence the 5 star rating, but is well worth the effort. Italian in origin, excellent food and bound to impress any guests.

£1.59 /PERSON

5

2

PREP 30 MINS

COOK 25 MINS

1 tablespoon **oil** to fry

1/2 **onion**, chopped

1 clove **garlic**, chopped

handful of **spinach**, torn into large pieces

300g pack of **cream cheese** (soft cheese)

2 tablespoons grated **Parmesan-style cheese**

8 **cannelloni shells**

2 extra tablespoons grated **Parmesan-style cheese**, for sprinkling on top

1 quantity of **Tomato Sauce** (see page 33). You could use the Quick Cheese Sauce on page 33 instead of the Tomato Sauce.

1. Preheat the oven to 180°C fan oven/200°C/Gas 6.

2. Make the Tomato Sauce (see page 33).

3. Heat the oil in a frying pan and fry the onion and garlic until the onions are soft. Add the spinach and cook until it wilts, approximately 1 minute.

4. Mix the cream cheese and Parmesan together in a bowl and soften with a fork. Add the onion and spinach mixture. Mix. Use this mixture to fill the cannelloni shells. Spoon into the top of the cannelloni tubes and push in with the handle of a small spoon. Repeat the process until the shell is completely full. Your hands will get very messy.

5. Place in a greased casserole dish or shallow, ovenproof dish and cover with the Tomato Sauce, or the Quick Cheese Sauce. Cook in the oven for 15 minutes. Sprinkle the rest of the Parmesan over the top and cook for another 10 minutes. Serve immediately.

Two Cheese and Spinach Loaf

You could spread this with butter and eat with more cheese and pickles. You could put half in the freezer, once it is cooled, as the loaf is quite big.

£2.73 /TOTAL

3

8

PREP 15 MINS

COOK 30 MINS

2cm cube **butter**

1 **leek**, chopped

¼ x 200g pack of fresh **spinach**

1½ mugs **self-raising flour**

salt and **pepper**

¾ mug **Parmesan-style cheese**

1 mug grated **Cheddar cheese**

1 teaspoon **basil**

1 **egg**, beaten + **milk** to make

¾ mug liquid

1. Preheat the oven to 180°C fan oven/200°C/Gas 6.

2. Heat the butter in a frying pan and fry the leeks. When they are soft, add the spinach and cook for about 30 seconds until it wilts.

3. In a bowl, mix the flour, salt and pepper, cheeses and basil. Add the leeks and spinach from the frying pan. Mix.

4. Add the egg and milk until it forms a ball in the bowl. You do not necessarily need to use all the liquid. It should not be too sticky.

5. Grease a loaf tin and then press the mixture evenly into it. Bake in the oven for 35–40 minutes. Once cooked, leave to cool and then slice.

Savoury Cheesecake

This is quite rich and therefore best served with a refreshing salad. Again, you could vary the vegetables which are included. Use mainly those you can grate: e.g. celeriac, sweet potato, butternut squash.

1 tablespoon **oil** to fry

2 large **potatoes**, cut into 1/2cm slices

1 **leek**, chopped

1 **pepper**, diced quite small

1 small **courgette**, grated

1 small **carrot**, grated

2 **eggs**

300g pack **cream cheese**

1/2 mug grated **Cheddar cheese**

1 teaspoon **chives**

salt and **pepper**

£1.68 /PERSON

4

2-3

PREP 20 MINS

COOK 25 MINS

1. Preheat the oven to 180°C fan oven/200°C/Gas 6. Grease a casserole dish.

2. Heat the oil in a frying pan and fry the sliced potatoes until they are browned. Take out of the pan and set aside.

3. If necessary, add more oil to the pan. Fry the leek, pepper, courgette and carrot.

4. Beat the eggs in a bowl and add the cheeses. Mix well. Add the chives and fried veg to the bowl. Season well and mix together.

5. Place the fried potatoes on the bottom of a casserole dish to form a base. Pour the cheese and vegetable mixture over the top.

6. Bake in the oven for 20–25 minutes until the cheese and egg mixture is set, but not too hard! It will brown a little. Serve with fresh salad.

Fajitas

This is a recipe for a basic fajita. On the opposite page are some ideas for variations. Fajitas have become so cosmopolitan that the fillings are no longer restricted to Mexican flavours. Serve them with salsa (see page 147).

£ **1.41** /PERSON

2

1

PREP **15 MINS**

1 tablespoon **oil** to fry

1/2 **onion**, sliced

1 small clove of **garlic**, chopped

1/2 red or **green pepper**, sliced

1 small **courgette**, thinly sliced

2 **mushrooms**, sliced

1/4 teaspoon **chilli flakes**

1 tablespoon **tomato purée**, mixed with 2 tablespoons **water**

2 **tortilla wraps**

1. Heat the oil in a frying pan. Fry the onion and the garlic for 1 minute, then add the peppers, courgettes and mushrooms and cook for 3–4 minutes until they are tender.

2. Add the chilli flakes, tomato purée and water. Stir well and cook for another 2–3 minutes to allow the flavours to mix.

3. Warm the tortillas under the grill for about 1 minute. Put half the mixture onto each of the tortilla wraps, roll them up and eat!

Variations for Fajitas

Different vegetables, etc. To add at stage 1

courgettes, cut into thin strips

mangetout or **sugar snaps**, cut into 2

peas, **sweetcorn** or baby corn cobs

beans sprouts

celery

butternut squash, precook for 10 minutes

beans: cannellini, pinto, haricot, etc.

spinach

roasted peppers; you can buy them in jars or roast them yourself (page 21).

tomatoes

pine nuts

Ideas for sauces. Add at stage 2

1 teaspoon **chilli sauce**

1 teaspoon **HP sauce**

1 dessertspoon **tomato sauce**

1 teaspoon **hoisin sauce**

1 tablespoon **vegetarian pesto** + 1 teaspoon **water**, or 1 tablespoon **cream**

1/2 teaspoon **curry paste** + 1 teaspoon **water**

Cheeses to add at the end of stage 3

feta, crumbled

goat's cheese

grated **Cheddar**

Quick Cheese Sauce, to pour over (see page 33)

tofu, cut into cubes and add at the end of the cooking time.

Serve with

salsa (see page 147)

yogurt

different **sauces** (see pages 32 & 33)

Nachos

Nachos are so quick to make and are excellent for parties or snacks while you are relaxing, watching a video, etc.

¹/2 x 200g packet of **corn chips**, plain or flavoured

1¹/2 mugs of grated **cheese**

dipping salsa sauce (see page 147)

£1.16 /PERSON

1

2-3

PREP 10 MINS

COOK 3 MINS

1. Heat the oven to 220°C fan oven/240°C/Gas 9.
2. Pile the chips on an ovenproof plate.
3. Sprinkle the grated cheese on the top and cover the chips.
4. Place in the oven for 2–3 minutes only. The cheese only needs to melt, it does not need to brown.
5. Pour the salsa over the top, serve and eat immediately.

Salsa

If you are having a party, these will work out much cheaper than the bought variety. Salsa is good with tortilla chips, quesidillas, and big wraps. If you like your salsa really hot, then adjust the amount of chilli powder or chilli flakes.

Dipping Salsa
£0.94 TOTAL

1 tablespoon **oil** to fry

1 **onion**, finely chopped

3 **cloves garlic**, finely chopped

400g tin of **chopped tomatoes**

1/2 tablespoon **tomato purée**

1 teaspoon **chilli flakes**

1/2 teaspoon **paprika**

1 teaspoon **sugar**

2 teaspoons **dried chives**

1. Heat a little oil in a saucepan and fry the onions and garlic in a pan, until they begin to brown.

2. Add the tin of tomatoes and bring to the boil. Add the tomato purée, chilli, paprika and sugar. Simmer gently for 3–4 minutes. Add the chives.

Avocado Salsa
£1.78 TOTAL

1 medium **avocado**, peeled and chopped into small pieces

1 medium **onion**, finely chopped

2 medium **tomatoes**, chopped into small pieces

1/2 teaspoon **chilli powder**

1/4 teaspoon **paprika**

1/2 teaspoon **sugar**

1 teaspoon **lemon juice** (this stops the avocado from discolouring)

salt and **pepper**

Tomato and Onion Salsa
£0.96 TOTAL

4 **tomatoes**, cut into small pieces

1 **green chilli pepper**, chopped finely

1/2 **onion**, chopped finely

1 teaspoon **sugar**

1 teaspoon **lemon juice**

salt and **pepper**

For Avocado Salsa and Tomato and Onion Salsa, simply prepare the ingredients and mix together.

Big Wraps

You will need to eat these with a knife and fork. It's not really possible with your fingers, but you could always give it a go if you don't mind the mess!

1 tablespoon **oil** to fry

1 **onion**, finely chopped

4 **mushrooms**, cut into fairly small pieces

1 red, green or yellow **pepper**, chopped

1/2 x 350g **chicken-style Quorn**

1/2 mug of cooked **rice** (see page 22)

1 small tin of **sweetcorn**

4 **tortilla wraps**

1/2 mug of finely grated strong **Cheddar cheese**

salt and **pepper**

a few **cocktail sticks**

salsa (see page 147)

1 dessertspoon **soured cream** (optional)

£1.15 /PERSON

2

4

PREP 25 MINS

1. Heat a little oil in a wok and fry the onions for 2–3 minutes until they begin to soften. Add the mushrooms and pepper and continue to cook for about 3 minutes.

2. Add the Quorn and cook for 1 minute.

3. Add the rice and the drained sweetcorn and cook for 2–3 minutes until everything is heated through. Season with salt and pepper. Take off the heat and leave in the pan to keep warm.

4. Gently warm the tortilla wraps under the grill on a low heat for 2 minutes, or in the microwave for 10 seconds.

5. Put 1/4 of the filling onto each wrap and sprinkle the grated cheese on the top. Place a blob of the soured cream on top. Fold the tortilla over and secure with a cocktail stick. Serve with the salsa.

Roast Wedges

This dish of oven-baked vegetables makes a good accompaniment to bean burgers, or vegetarian sausages, but can make a meal in itself.

1 large **potato**, cut into wedges

¹/2 **yellow** or **red pepper**, sliced

2 **mushrooms**, sliced

2 **tomatoes**, cut into wedges

1 tablespoon **tomato purée**

1 teaspoon **chives**

¹/4 mug **water**
+ 1 **vegetable stock cube**

salt and **pepper**

¹/2 mug grated **cheese**

£0.81 /PERSON

2

2

PREP
10 MINS

COOK
20 MINS

1. Preheat the oven to 180°C fan oven/200°C/Gas 6.

2. Put the potato into a pan of boiling water, then simmer for 10 minutes. Drain and put into a greased casserole dish.

3. Add the peppers, mushrooms and tomatoes.

4. Mix the tomato purée, chives, water and crumbled stock cube together in a mug or small bowl. Pour over the vegetables and mix. Season well.

5. Top with grated cheese and place in the oven for 15-20 minutes until the cheese is browned.

Curried Wedges

This is how to make chips the safe way, without deep frying. Also, they are slightly more healthy. If you don't want your chips spicy, just wedges, don't add the curry paste to the oil.

1 large **sweet potato**

2 large **potatoes**

¼ mug **oil**

1 teaspoon **curry paste**

£0.60 /PERSON

2

2

PREP 10 MINS

COOK 40 MINS

1. Preheat the oven to 180°C fan oven/200°C/Gas 6.

2. Peel the sweet potato. You do not need to peel the ordinary potatoes, just wash them. Cut them all into chips.

3. Place the chips on a baking tray. Using a mug, mix the curry paste with the oil and sprinkle over the chips. Toss the chips in the oil to make sure they are all covered. Spread them out on the tray.

4. Cook in the oven for 40 minutes. They should be nicely browned by this point.

Leek and Cheese Rolls

It is a good idea to keep a packet of frozen pastry in your freezer drawer.

£0.32 /EACH

3

16

PREP 25 MINS

COOK 15 MINS

375g pack ready-rolled **flaky pastry**

1 small **leek**, sliced

2cm cube **butter**

2 slices **wholemeal bread**, made into breadcrumbs

4 **egg yolks**

1 teaspoon **mustard**

1 teaspoon **dried thyme**

1½ mugs strong **Cheddar cheese**, grated

salt and **pepper**

1 beaten **egg**

1. Preheat the oven on 200°C fan oven/220°C/Gas 7. Grease a baking tray.

2. Fry the leeks in the butter. Once softened a little, place in a bowl.

3. Add the breadcrumbs, egg yolks, mustard, cheese, thyme. Mix together and season well.

4. Unroll the sheet of pastry and cut in half, lengthways. Dampen one edge of each piece of the pastry to help it stick together.

5. Divide the mixture between the two pieces of pastry and form into two long sausages. Fold the pastry over and pinch the edges together. Cut each sausage into eight and place on the baking tray. Brush with the beaten egg.

6. Place in the oven for 12–15 minutes until the rolls are browned.

Nutty Sweet Potato and Spinach Pie

Spinach only takes seconds to cook. As soon as it has wilted, take it out of the pan.

£3.33 /PERSON

4

2-3

PREP 20 MINS

COOK 20 MINS

375g pack of ready-rolled **shortcrust pastry**

2 large **sweet potatoes**, peeled and cut into chunks

2 x 2cm cube **butter**

1 tablespoon **oil** to fry

200g pack **fresh spinach**

1 tablespoon **oil** to fry

2 **onions**, sliced

100g pack **pine nuts**

2 teaspoons **fennel seeds**

1 teaspoon **honey**

1 **egg**, beaten

salt and **pepper**

1. Preheat the oven to 200°C fan oven/220°C/Gas 7. Grease a 20cm x 13cm casserole dish.

2. Boil the sweet potatoes for 10–15 minutes. Drain and mash with 2cm cube of butter and salt and pepper. Set to one side until needed.

3. Heat a little oil in a wok and add the spinach. Cook for no more than one minute. The spinach will wilt. Place the spinach on the bottom of the casserole dish.

4. Heat the other 2cm cube of butter and the oil in the wok. Add the sliced onions and pine nuts and fry until they begin to turn brown. Stir frequently. Add the fennel seeds and honey and fry for 30 seconds. Season with salt and pepper.

5. Place the mashed sweet potato on top of the spinach in the casserole dish. Spread evenly.

6. Place the onion mix on top of the sweet potato.

7. Unroll the pastry and cut a piece big enough to cover the top of the casserole dish. Place on the dish and pinch the edges. Brush with the beaten egg and place in the oven for 20 minutes until the pastry is golden brown.

152 friends around

Spinach and Cottage Cheese Lasagna

You could add an extra teaspoon of flour to the cheese sauce mix to make it less runny and the lasagna will hold together better.

£1.91 /PERSON

5

3-4

PREP
30 MINS

COOK
25 MINS

2 x **Quick Cheese Sauce** (page 33)

450g **cottage cheese**

1/2 mug grated **Cheddar cheese**

oil to fry

1 small **onion**, chopped

1 **clove garlic**, finely chopped

500g **fresh spinach**

juice of a 1/2 **lemon**

salt and **pepper**

250g pack of **lasagna sheets**

1/2 mug grated **Cheddar cheese** for the top

crusty bread to serve

1. Preheat the oven to 180°C fan oven/200°C/Gas 6. Grease a casserole dish.

2. Make the Quick Cheese Sauce (see page 33).

3. Mix together 1/2 mug grated cheese and the cottage cheese.

4. Heat a little oil in a frying pan or wok and add the onions and garlic. Fry until the onions begin to soften. Add the spinach and fry until it begins to wilt. Take off the heat, add the lemon juice and season well with salt and pepper.

5. Put some of the cheese sauce in the bottom of the casserole dish, then a single layer of lasagna sheets, then add the cottage cheese mix, then another layer of lasagna sheets, then a layer of cheese sauce and finally another layer of lasagna sheets. Place the spinach mix on top, followed by another layer of lasagna sheets. Top with cheese sauce and lastly, the other 1/2 mug of grated cheese.

6. Place in the oven for 25 minutes. The cheese should be browned on the top and the lasagna sheets cooked.

7. Serve with crusty bread.

For another angle on the classic lasagna, why not try Joy's Mushroom Lasagna. The recipe is over at noshbooks.com/mushroom

comfort food

Want something to give you that warm, 'cosy' feeling, without spending too much money? Have yourself something wholesome.

Leek and Potato Soup

The recipe asks for double cream, but you can replace this with milk. It freezes well for another day.

2cm cube **butter** to fry

2 **leeks**, sliced

1 small **potato**, diced

1 small **carrot**, chopped

3 mugs **water** with 2 vegetable **stock cubes** crumbled in

salt and **pepper** to taste

2 tablespoons **double cream**

£0.66 /PERSON

2

2

PREP 10 MINS

COOK 20 MINS

1. Melt the butter in a saucepan and fry the vegetables for 4–5 minutes. Stir frequently.

2. Add the stock and water and bring to the boil. Turn down the heat and simmer for 15 minutes.

3. Using the hand-held blender, whizz until the soup is smooth.

4. Stir in the double cream and season with salt and pepper. Serve with crusty bread.

Classic Nut Roast

You can use a variety of nuts in this recipe, but cashews, macadamia or Brazil nuts seem to work the best. Any leftovers are ideal to eat cold the next day, probably best not microwaved.

£1.29 /PERSON

2

2

PREP 10 MINS

COOK 20 MINS

1 tablespoon **oil** to fry

1 small **onion**, chopped finely

2 **mushrooms**, chopped finely

200g pack **cashew nuts**, chopped

2 slices **wholemeal bread**

$^1/_2$ mug boiling **water**

$^1/_4$ mug **vegetable stock**

1 teaspoon **Marmite**

1 teaspoon **mixed herbs**

1. Preheat the oven to 180°C fan oven/200°C/Gas 6. Grease a small ovenproof dish. You can use your casserole dish.

2. Fry the onions in a little oil in a saucepan until they begin to brown. Add the mushrooms and cook for a further 2–3 minutes. Take off the heat.

3. Add the chopped nuts to the pan.

4. Make the bread into breadcrumbs. Just rub it between your fingers; it does not matter if the breadcrumbs are a bit chunky. Add to the pan.

5. Add $^1/_2$ vegetable stock cube into $^1/_2$ a mug of boiling water to make up the stock. Add the teaspoon of Marmite and stir until dissolved.

6. Add the herbs and the contents of the mug to the pan. Mix everything together.

7. Pour into the dish and cook for 20 minutes in the oven. The nuts should be brown on top.

8. Serve with salad, baked potatoes, pasta, or roasted vegetables. If you wish, serve with one of the sauces on pages 32 & 33.

Curried Split Pea Casserole

You need to decide on this one ahead of time, since the peas need to be soaked overnight and the cooking time is lengthy. The actual labour time is not. You can reheat any leftovers the next day.

£1.21 /PERSON

2

2-3

PREP 15 MINS

COOK 60 MINS

1 tablespoon **oil** to fry

1 small **onion**, chopped

1 teaspoon grated **ginger**

1 clove of **garlic**, chopped

1 small **carrot**, grated

1/3 mug **yellow split peas**, soaked overnight

1 teaspoon **wholegrain mustard**

1 small **red chilli**, deseeded and chopped

1 dessertspoon **curry paste**

1 dessertspoon **tomato purée**

400g tin of **chopped tomatoes**

1 mug of **water** + 1 vegetable **stock cube**

2 **sweet potatoes**, peeled and cut into chunks

1 **courgette**, sliced

1 teaspoon **chopped chives**

salt and **pepper**

naan bread, crusty bread or **rice** (see page 22) to serve

1. Heat the oil in a saucepan. Add the onion, ginger, garlic and carrots. Cook for about 5 minutes until soft.

2. Add the peas, mustard, chilli, curry paste, tomato purée, tinned tomatoes, water and crumbled stock cubes. Bring to the boil and season well. Turn the heat down and simmer for about 40 minutes.

3. Add the squash and the courgette. Simmer for a further 20 minutes until the squash is tender. Stir the chives in, right at the end. Season well with salt and pepper.

4. Eat whilst still warm. Serve with naan bread, crusty bread or rice (see page 22).

Cannellini Bean Casserole

Eat it on its own, or with baked potatoes, rice or crusty bread. You can vary the beans used and add other vegetables if you wish. They will need to be quick-cook vegetables, such as mushrooms, or courgettes, not root vegetables.

1 tablespoon **oil** to fry

3 small **shallots** (very small onions), sliced

1 clove **garlic**, chopped

1 stick **celery**, chopped

3 medium **tomatoes**, cut into chunks

1/2 mug **water** + 1 **vegetable stock cube**

400g tin **cannellini beans**, rinsed and drained

1 dessertspoon **tomato purée**

1/2 teaspoon **Tobasco sauce**, more if you like things spicy

salt and **pepper**

1. Heat the oil in a saucepan and fry the shallots, garlic and celery for 2 minutes. Add the tomatoes and cook for a further 2 minutes. Add the water and crumbled stock cube and cook for another 1 minute.

2. Add the beans, tomato purée and the Tobasco sauce. Bring to the boil. Turn the heat down and cook for 2–3 minutes to heat the beans through. Season well and serve.

Winter Warming Hot Pot

This is a good basic recipe. You can add and subtract vegetables as you have them to hand. You can also replace the Marmite with different flavourings: chilli, curry paste, mustard, etc. You need to have a good variety within the pot for it to taste good. Serve with crusty bread or baked potatoes. Reheats well the next day.

£0.87 /PERSON

1

2-3

PREP 10 MINS

COOK 20 MINS

1 small **onion**, chopped

1 **carrot**, peeled and chopped into small chunks

1 **parsnip**, peeled and chopped into small chunks

1/4 **swede**, peeled and chopped into chunks

1/4 **celeriac**, peeled and chopped into small chunks

1 **courgette**, sliced

2 sticks **celery**, sliced

400g tin **pinto beans** or **black-eyed beans**, drained and rinsed

1 mug **water** + 1 vegetable **stock cube**, crumbled

1 teaspoon **Marmite** or yeast extract

salt and **pepper**

1. Heat a little oil in a saucepan and fry the vegetables until they begin to brown a little.

2. Add the rest of the ingredients. Bring to the boil and then turn down to simmer for 20 minutes. Check to see that the vegetables are all cooked. Do not overcook them. Check the seasoning and add more salt and pepper if necessary.

comfort food **159**

Shepherd's Pie

No need to bother with mashed potatoes. If you want to cook it with Quorn mince, add after the vegetables in stage 2. Cook for a few minutes, before adding the tomatoes etc.

£0.88 /PERSON

2

2-3

PREP 15 MINS

COOK 25 MINS

1 tablespoon **oil** to fry

1/2 **onion**, chopped

1 small **carrot**, chopped

5 **mushrooms**, sliced

1 clove **garlic**, chopped

400g can **chopped tomatoes**

1/2 x 400ml can black-eyed or **cannellini beans**

2 teaspoons **HP sauce**, or 1/4 teaspoon **Tobasco sauce**

1 vegetable **stock cube**, crumbled

1 teaspoon **basil**

1 teaspoon **sugar**

Topping

2 large **potatoes**, diced

2cm cube **butter**

1/2 mug grated **Cheddar cheese**

1. Preheat the oven to 180°C fan oven/200°C/Gas 6. Put the diced potatoes on to boil for 10 minutes.

2. Heat the oil in a saucepan. Fry the onions, carrots, mushrooms and garlic. Allow them to brown a little. Add the tomatoes, beans, HP (or Tobasco sauce), stock cube, basil and sugar. Cook for 10 minutes until the vegetables are tender.

3. By now the potatoes should be cooked. Drain them and return them back into the pan. Add the butter and shake the pan, with the lid on until the butter is mixed. The potatoes should go a bit 'raggy' round the edges.

4. Put the bean mixture in a casserole dish and top with the potatoes. Sprinkle the cheese on top and bake in the oven for 25 minutes until the cheese has browned.

Chilli Bean Stew, with Crusty Bread

Reheats well, you can, of course vary the beans.

£1.65 /PERSON

1

2

PREP 20 MINS

1 tablespoon **oil** to fry

1 **onion**, sliced

1 clove **garlic**, finely chopped

1/2 **red pepper**, chopped

4–5 **mushrooms**, sliced

400g tin **chopped tomatoes**

1 vegetable **stock cube**

1/2 teaspoon **chilli flakes**

1 tablespoon **tomato purée**

1 teaspoon **sugar**

1/2 mug **water**

1/2 x 400g tin **aduki beans**, drained and rinsed

1/2 x 400g tin **black-eyed beans**, drained and rinsed

crusty bread to serve

1. Heat the oil in a wok. Add the onions and garlic and fry for 2–3 minutes. Add the peppers and mushrooms and fry for a further 2 minutes.

2. Add the tomatoes, stock, chilli flakes, tomato purée, sugar, water and beans. Bring to the boil and then simmer for 5 minutes.

comfort food **161**

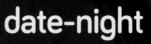

date-night

Need to impress that special someone without slogging in the kitchen for hours? Try some of these 'scrummy' recipes.

date night

Stuffed Aubergines

Aubergines are a good source of fibre and folic acid. Probably best bought June to September, when they are in season and a little cheaper.

1 large **aubergine**

1/2 x 200g **feta cheese**

10 **olives**, chopped

1/2 x 200g pack **pine nuts**

3 pieces **sun-dried tomato**, chopped

1/2 mug **Parmesan-style cheese**

salt and **pepper**

oil

1. Preheat the oven to 200°C fan oven/220°C/Gas 7. Lightly grease a baking tray.

2. Cut the aubergines in half and brush with oil. Place in the oven, for 20–25 minutes until the flesh in the middle is soft enough to scoop out.

3. Meanwhile, mix together the feta, olives, pine nuts and sun-dried tomatoes. Season well.

4. Once the aubergines are cooked, scoop out the soft flesh from the middle and mix together with the cheese mixture. Place back in the aubergine shells. Sprinkle over with grated Parmesan.

5. Place back in the oven for 10–15 minutes until the cheese is brown.

6. Serve with some salad.

Mushroom and Brie Pasta

Brie is, of course, a little more expensive than the usual Cheddar, but will make things that bit more special. Any excess will make a delicious sandwich, if you add some salad to it.

£1.44 /PERSON

2

2

PREP 20 MINS

1¹/2 mugs **pasta**

1 tablespoon **oil**

3 **spring onions**, chopped

2 cloves of **garlic**, finely chopped

8 medium **mushrooms**, sliced

1 vegetable **stock cube** crumbled into 4 tablespoons **water**

5 pieces **sun-dried tomatoes**, sliced

1 dessertspoon **wholegrain mustard**

4 tablespoons **double cream**

125g pack of **Brie**, cut into slices

salt and **pepper**

1. Put the pasta on to cook (see page 23).

2. Heat oil in a frying pan. Fry the spring onions, garlic and mushrooms until the mushrooms are soft.

3. Add the stock cube and water and simmer, uncovered, until almost all the stock has reduced.

4. Add the tomatoes, mustard, cream and cheese. Cook until the Brie has melted.

5. Stir in the cooked, drained pasta.

6. Season well and serve.

Pasta with Onions and Green Beans

The preparation time here is a bit lengthy, but not too difficult. The final result is a lovely sweet-and-sour flavour not usually associated with pasta dishes.

£1.62 /PERSON

3

1

PREP 30 MINS

$\frac{1}{2}$ x 200g pack **green beans**

1 tablespoon **oil** to fry

1 **red onion**, sliced

1 **garlic clove**, chopped

2 tablespoons **water**

1 tablespoon **raisins**

2 tablespoons **sugar**

2 tablespoons **red** or **white wine vinegar**

$\frac{1}{4}$ x 200g pack of **spinach**

one portion of **tagliatelle** (see page 23)

1. Put the beans in boiling water and simmer for 5 minutes. Drain and return to the pan.

2. Put the pasta on to cook (see page 23).

3. Heat a little oil in a frying pan and fry the onions and garlic for about 6–8 minutes. Stir frequently. They should be soft and quite brown.

4. Add the water, raisins, garlic, sugar and vinegar and cook for 2–3 minutes.

5. Add the spinach and cook until it wilts. Add the green beans.

6. Drain the pasta and put on a plate. Top with the onions and beans.

Mushroom Stroganoff

It is worth buying different varieties of mushroom to use in this dish. Shitake mushrooms have a great flavour and are not too expensive.

£1.22 /PERSON

★ 1

🍴 2

PREP 15 MINS

1 tablespoon **oil** to fry

1 small **onion**, chopped finely

2 **celery sticks**, sliced finely

12 medium **mushrooms**, sliced

1 dessertspoon **flour**

1 vegetable **stock cube**,

dissolved in ½ mug **water**

1 dessertspoon **chives**

2 tablespoons **soured cream**

salt and **pepper**

rice to serve (see page 22)

1. Put the oil in the pan and fry the onions and celery until they are transparent.

2. Add a little more oil to the pan, add the mushrooms and cook for 1 minute.

3. Add the flour to the pan. Mix together and then add the crumbled stock cube and water. Bring to the boil, then turn down the heat and simmer, uncovered, for 1 minute.

4. Take off the heat and add the soured cream and the chives. Season with salt and pepper. Serve with rice (see page 22).

Creamy Parmesan-Style Pasta

If you wish, you could add mushrooms to this recipe.

2 mugs of **pasta**

3cm cube **butter**

5 **spring onions**, chopped

1 small clove **garlic**, finely chopped

100g pack **pine nuts**

1/2 mug **frozen peas**

1 mug **double cream** or 3/4 x 300ml carton

1/2 teaspoon **nutmeg**

salt and **pepper**

1 mug **grated Parmesan-style cheese**

£2.35 /PERSON

2

2

PREP 25 MINS

1. Put the pasta on to cook (see page 23). Drain and leave in the pan.

2. Heat the butter in a frying pan and add the onions, garlic and pine nuts. Fry until the onions begin to soften and brown.

3. Add the frozen peas to the pan and stir.

4. Add the cream and the nutmeg and bring to the boil. Stir in the grated Parmesan and drained pasta. Take off the heat immediately. Season well with salt and pepper.

Peppers Stuffed with Feta and Pine Nuts

Cut some of the lumpy bits off the bottoms of the peppers so they 'stand up' on the tray.

£2.43 /PERSON

3

2

PREP 10 MINS

COOK 25 MINS

2 large **red** or **yellow peppers**

1/4 mug **couscous** + 1/2 mug boiling **water** + 1 vegetable **stock cube**

1 tablespoon **olive oil**

4 **spring onions**, chopped

4–6 ready-to-eat **dried apricots**, chopped

200g **feta cheese**, crumbled

2 medium **tomatoes**, chopped finely

1/2 x 100g pack **pine nuts**

1 tablespoon freshly chopped **basil**

salt and **pepper**

1. Preheat the oven to 180°C fan oven/200°C/Gas 6. Grease a baking tray.

2. Cut the tops off each and scoop out the seeds and the veins. Stand on the tray.

3. Put the couscous in a bowl with the boiling water and stock cube. Cover with a plate and leave to soak for 4–5 minutes. All the water should have been absorbed.

4. Add the rest of the ingredients and mix together. Season with pepper. The feta is quite salty so don't add more.

5. Fill the peppers with the mixture. Put them on the baking tray and place them in the oven for 25 minutes. The tops should be nicely browned.

6. Serve with salad, or mini roast potatoes (see photo).

Mushroom and Cashew Nut Pasta

You can boil the green beans and pasta in one pan, if you time it carefully.
Just put the beans in 6 minutes before the end of the cooking time for the pasta.

1 mug of **pasta**

1 tablespoon **oil** to fry

200g pack **green beans**, cut in half

1 **onion**, sliced

1 clove **garlic**, finely chopped

5-6 **mushrooms**, sliced

100g pack **cashew nuts**

350ml pot of **crème fraîche** or **soured cream**

1 vegetable **stock cube**

½ mug grated **Parmesan-style cheese**

£2.17 /PERSON

2

2

PREP 25 MINS

1. Put the pasta on to boil (see page 23).

2. Put the green beans on to boil and turn down to simmer for 5-6 minutes. Drain and set to one side until needed.

3. Heat the oil in a wok and fry the onions and garlic until the onions are soft.

4. Add the mushrooms and cashew nuts and fry for 1 minute.

5. Add the crème fraîche and the crumbled stock cube. Cook for 30 seconds, mixing everything together.

6. Add the drained pasta and beans and cook on a medium heat for 1–2 minutes until everything is hot.

7. Stir in the Parmesan and serve.

Sweet and Sour Quorn

You can use this sweet and sour sauce with other recipes.

£1.56 /PERSON

2

2

PREP 25 MINS

Sweet and Sour Sauce

1 tablespoon **sugar**

1 dessertspoon **cornflour**

2 tablespoons **wine vinegar**

1 tablespoon **soy sauce**

1 tablespoon **tomato purée**

3/4 mug **water**

rice to serve (see page 22)

1 tablespoon **oil** to fry

1/2 **onion**, sliced

1 clove **garlic**, finely chopped

1/2 **red pepper**, sliced

1/2 x 300g packet of **chicken-style Quorn pieces**

1/4 x 250g pack **mangetout**, each cut into 4

227g tin **pineapple chunks**, drained

1. Mix the sauce ingredients together. Leave to one side until needed.

2. Heat the oil in a wok or large saucepan. Add the onions, garlic, peppers and Quorn. Fry for 1 minute.

3. Add the mangetout and pineapple chunks to the pan. Fry for 1 minute.

4. Add the sauce and bring to the boil.

5. Turn down to simmer for 1 minute.

6. Serve with rice (see page 22).

Cheesy Caesar Salad

If you leave the peeled avocado uncovered, it will soon turn brown. Once the dressing is poured over it, it is OK.

£1.65 /PERSON

PREP 20 MINS

1 tablespoon **oil** to fry

1 slice **wholemeal bread**

1 small **cos lettuce**, cut into strips

4 **spring onions**, cut into long strips

1 **avocado**, peeled and cut into thin wedges

5cm piece of **cucumber**, cut into strips

1/2 x 200g pack **feta cheese**

1/2 mug grated **Parmesan-style cheese**

Dressing

2 tablespoons **olive oil**

1 tablespoon **mayo**

1 teaspoon **wholegrain mustard**

1 teaspoon **sugar**

salt and **pepper**

1. Prepare the dressing by mixing the ingredients together.

2. Heat a little oil in a frying pan and fry the slice of bread until it is browned on both sides. Cut into cubes.

3. Mix together the lettuce, spring onions, avocado, fried bread and cucumber. Add the dressing and mix well.

4. Crumble the feta on top of the salad and sprinkle the Parmesan over. Ready to eat!

cakes & cookies

Looking for some comforting nibbles?
Try a few of these and share them with friends.

Dream Bars

You can vary the actual nuts and the seeds you use, just keep to the same amounts. Be careful to stick to the timing at stage 3, otherwise the bars will not set.

£ 0.17 /EACH

3

20

PREP 15 MINS

COOL 1 HOUR

1 mug ready-to-eat **dried apricots**, chopped

3/4 mug **desiccated coconut**

1/2 x 100g pack of **toasted, flaked almonds**

1/2 x 100g pack of **sunflower** or

pumpkin seeds

3 1/2 mugs **Rice Krispies**

100g **butter** (measure using packet)

2/3 mug **brown sugar**

2 rounded tablespoons **golden syrup**

1. Grease a baking tray and put a piece of greaseproof paper in the bottom.

2. Put the apricots, coconut, nuts, pumpkin seeds and Rice Krispies in a bowl. Mix together.

3. Put the butter, sugar and syrup in a pan and melt. Simmer briskly for 1 1/2 minutes. The sugar should all be dissolved and the mixture will be like toffee. The sugar is very hot at this point, so take care.

4. Pour immediately into the dry ingredients in the bowl. Mix fairly quickly and thoroughly, making sure that there are no dry patches.

5. Turn out into the baking tray. Press down so that it sticks together and spreads out. Leave for about 1 hour to set and cool. Cut into pieces and eat.

Muffins

Muffins are really quick and easy to make and there are many variations. There are a few listed here.

3 mugs **self-raising flour**

1 mug **brown sugar** (you can use white)

2 **eggs**, slightly beaten

1½ mugs **milk**

¾ mug **vegetable oil**

£0.11 /MUFFIN

2

12

PREP 15 MINS

COOK 20 MINS

1. Preheat the oven to 180°C fan oven/200°C/Gas 6.

2. Mix the flour and sugar in a bowl.

3. Add the eggs, milk and oil into the bowl. Stir together. The mixture will be a bit lumpy, but do not overmix.

4. If you have cake tins, use them and put paper cake cases in each hole. If you do not have cake tins, put double paper cake cases for each muffin on your baking tray. This will help the cases hold their shape. Spoon the mixture into each case.

5. Bake in the oven for 20 minutes. If you use the larger muffin cases, you will need to bake them for 25 minutes. They should be a little brown and spring back when gently pressed.

Variations

Once you have the hang of these variations, you can experiment with your own varieties. Don't put anything too wet into the ingredients and don't add more liquid. If you want to add something very wet, then reduce the quantity of milk by a proportional amount.

Summers fruits

Just add 1/2 x 500g bag of frozen, defrosted and drained, **summer fruits** to the wet ingredients. Bake as usual.

Apple

Add 2 cooking or **eating apples**, cored and chopped up, + 1 teaspoon **cinnamon** to the dry ingredients.

Dates

Add 1 mug chopped **dates**, 2 teaspoons **ground ginger**, 1/2 teaspoon **cinnamon** and the grated **rind of an orange** to the dry ingredients.

Nuts

Add 1 mug chopped **pecan nuts** + 2 teaspoons **instant coffee grains** to the dry ingredients.

White chocolate and berry

Add 100g pack of **white chocolate chips** and 1/2 x 500g pack frozen **fruits of the forest** along with the wet ingredients.

Apricot and marmalade

Replace 1/2 mug **flour** with 1/2 mug **muesli**. Add 100g **ready-to-eat apricots**, chopped and the grated **rind of 1 orange** to the dry ingredients. When the mixture is in the cases, but before it goes into the oven, drop 1 teaspoon of **marmalade** into the centre of each muffin. Bake as usual.

Honey and oats

Replace 1/2 mug of flour with 1/2 mug **oats** and add 1/2 teaspoon **cinnamon** and 1/2 mug **raisins** to the dry ingredients and 2 tablespoons of honey to the wet ingredients.

Banana and nut

Squash 2 large **bananas** and add when the mixture is wet, together with 1/2 mug **chopped nuts**.

Cranberry and poppy seed

Add 4 teaspoons **poppy seeds** to the dry ingredients and a 140g pack of **dried cranberries** to the wet ingredients.

Chocolate chip muffins

Add two 100g packets of **chocolate chips**. Two different varieties work well; for example, white and milk or plain chocolate. If you want double choc chip muffins, instead of the 3 mugs of flour, use $2^2/3$ **flour** and 1/3 mug **drinking chocolate**.

Cashew Nut Cookies

Creamed coconut is usually found in the 'Oriental foods' section at the supermarket.

150g softened **butter** (measure using packet)

$2/3$ mug **brown sugar**

1 **egg**

200g pack **cashew nuts**, roughly chopped

$1/2$ x 200g packet of **creamed coconut**, grated

1 mug **self-raising flour**

1 dessertspoon ground **ginger** (optional)

£0.21 /EACH

3

16

PREP 20 MINS

COOK 15 MINS

1. Preheat the oven to 180°C fan oven/200°C/Gas 6.
2. Cream the butter and sugar in a bowl and beat in the egg.
3. Add the rest of the ingredients and mix well.
4. Tip out onto a floured surface and squash into a long sausage. The dough is quite sticky. Cut into 16 and make each shape into a round, but do not squash too flat.
5. Place on a greased baking tray (you can cook in batches if you only have one tray). Bake in the oven for 15 minutes. The cookies should go golden brown.

Cakes and cookies

Nutty Honey Cake

This will keep for a week, if kept in a tin or a sealed bag. Good way of using up over-ripe bananas.

1 large **banana**

2 **eggs**

3 tablespoons **honey**

1/3 x 250g pack stoned **dates**, chopped

3/4 mug **brown sugar**

50g pack of **pecan nuts** (other varieties are OK)

150g **butter** (measure using packet)

11/2 mugs **self-raising flour**

1/2 teaspoon **cinnamon**

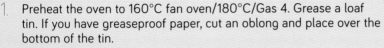

£0.25 /PERSON

2

12

PREP 15 MINS

COOK 60 MINS

1. Preheat the oven to 160°C fan oven/180°C/Gas 4. Grease a loaf tin. If you have greaseproof paper, cut an oblong and place over the bottom of the tin.

2. Peel and mash the banana in a fairly large bowl.

3. Add the eggs and beat together. Add the honey, dates, sugar and the nuts. Mix well.

4. Melt the butter over a low heat in a pan, then stir into the mixture in the bowl.

5. Add the flour and the cinnamon to the bowl. Mix well, but do not beat vigorously. Pour into the loaf tin.

6. Cook in the oven for 1 hour. The cake should spring back when pressed gently on the top.

Cherry Cookies

Don't eat straight away as the cherries are very hot!

250g block **butter**, softened

$^2/_3$ mug **sugar**

200g pack of **cochineal free glacé cherries**

2 tablespoons **mixed fruit** or **raisins**

1 mug **self-raising flour**

2 mugs **oats**

£ 0.17 /EACH

3

18

PREP 20 MINS

COOK 20 MINS

1. Preheat the oven to 160°C fan oven/180°C/Gas 4.

2. Using a wooden spoon, cream the softened butter and sugar together in a bowl until they are light and fluffy. This may take a few minutes.

3. Stir in the whole cherries, flour, fruit and oats. It seems at first as though it will not mix in, but it does.

4. Tip the mixture onto a floured surface and squeeze together. Divide into approx. 18 pieces and roll into balls. Grease a baking tray and squash the balls down, so they are just over 2cm thick. They will spread a bit when you cook them, so place them apart. Cook in the oven for 15–20 minutes. They should go golden brown.

Nutty Fruit Squares

Keep in a sealed box or tin and these will make great additions to your lunch for a few days.

£0.23 /EACH

3

18

PREP 20 MINS

COOK 45 MINS

2 medium **eating apples** chopped

³/4 mug **brown sugar**

2 teaspoons **cinnamon**

2 mugs **self-raising flour**

³/4 mug **dates**, cut into pieces

¹/2 x 200g pack **Brazil nuts**, roughly

200g **butter** (measure using packet)

3 **eggs**, beaten

extra 2 tablespoons **brown sugar** for the top

1. Preheat the oven to 180°C fan oven/200°C/Gas 6. Grease a baking tray and put some greaseproof paper over the bottom.

2. Core the apples and cut into fairly small chunks. Put them in a bowl with the sugar, cinnamon, flour, dates and nuts.

3. Melt the butter on a low heat. When it has cooled a little, add to the eggs and gently beat. Pour this into the dry ingredients in the bowl. The mixture is quite dry, so needs to be mixed well.

4. Press evenly into a baking tray, to make it level. Sprinkle the 2 tablespoons of brown sugar evenly over the top. Bake in the oven for 40–45 minutes. Leave to cool and cut into squares.

Orange Chocolate Cake

You will need to buy a cake tin if you want to make this one. It would make a great birthday cake for someone.

100g **dark chocolate**

3 **oranges**

3 **eggs**

3/4 mug **sunflower oil**

1 1/4 mugs **sugar**

1 1/2 mugs **self-raising flour**

3 tablespoons **cocoa**

Topping

200g **dark chocolate**

1 mug **double cream**

£0.30 /SLICE

4

16

PREP 20 MINS

COOK 55 MINS

1. Preheat the oven to 160°C fan oven/180°C/Gas 5. Grease a 24cm cake tin and put a circle of greaseproof paper in the bottom.

2. Break up 100g of chocolate and melt, gently, in a bowl over a saucepan of simmering water. Once melted, take off the heat.

3. Grate the rind from one of the oranges. Place in a mixing bowl. Cut the rind off all 3 oranges and put the flesh in the bowl with the grated rind. Whizz with the blender.

4. Beat the eggs and add to the bowl, with the oil and sugar. Beat well.

5. By now the chocolate should have cooled a little, so add to the bowl and mix well.

6. Add the flour and the cocoa. Mix well, but do not beat. The mixture will be very wet, don't worry! Pour the mixture into the cake tin and bake in the oven for 50-55 minutes. The cake should spring back when gently pressed.

7. To make the topping, put the cream in a saucepan and bring to the boil. Immediately take off the heat. Break up 200g chocolate, add to the cream and stir until it melts. Leave to cool and it will start to set. Once the cake has cooled and the topping has begun to set, spread it over the top. Serve on its own, or with cream.

For something a bit more colourful, check out a cake Joy made with Bella, her grandaughter, at noshbooks.com/bella-cake

Pine Nut Cookies

To make creaming the butter and sugar easy, chop the butter into small pieces and leave out of the fridge for an hour or so. This will make it soft and easy to mix.

125g softened **butter** (measure using packet)

²/₃ mug **sugar**

1 **egg**

1¹/₂ mugs **self-raising flour**

¹/₂ mug **pine nuts**

£ 0.20 /EACH

★ 3

🍴 18

PREP 15 MINS

COOK 15 MINS

COOL ¹/₂ HR

1. In a bowl, cream the butter and sugar together with a wooden spoon. Add the egg and beat well.

2. Add the flour and the nuts and mix well. It will be a little stiff. Keep a few nuts for stage 6.

3. Press into a sausage shape about 30cm long and cover with cling film. Leave in the fridge for half an hour.

4. Preheat the oven to 160°C fan oven/180°C/Gas 4.

5. Cut the sausage into 16 or 18 pieces and squash each cookie into a round. Squash down to about 2cm thick.

6. Place them on a greased baking tray and put a couple of pine nuts on each one. Bake in the oven for 12-15 minutes. They should go golden brown.

Oat Crunchies

If you only have one baking tray, it is OK to leave half the mixture standing while you cook the first half.

1 mug **rolled oats**

1 mug **desiccated coconut**

1 mug **self-raising flour**

1/2 mug **sugar**

100g **butter** (measure using packet)

1 heaped tablespoon **golden syrup**

3 tablespoons **water**

£0.05 /EACH

2

24

PREP 15 MINS

COOK 12 MINS

1. Preheat the oven to 180°C fan oven/200°C/Gas 6.

2. Put all the dry ingredients in a bowl.

3. Melt the butter in a pan on a low heat. Add the syrup and the water and stir.

4. Pour into the dry ingredients and mix well.

5. Grease a baking tray. Take about a tablespoon of the mixture at a time, squeeze into a ball and place on the baking sheet. Squash down gently. Place them a little apart, since they will spread as they cook. Put about 8 on the tray.

6. Bake for 10-12 minutes until golden brown.

Nut and Apricot Bars

These make good alternatives to some of the more expensive fruit bars you can buy in the supermarket.

£0.17 /EACH

3

18

PREP 15 MINS

COOK 30 MINS

1 medium **cooking apple**, chopped

2 tablespoons **sugar**

1/4 mug **water**

100g pack of **toasted, flaked almonds**

3/4 mug **porridge oats**

2/3 mug **self-raising flour**

11/3 mugs ready-to-eat **apricots**, chopped

2 **eggs**, beaten

2 tablespoons **sunflower oil**

2 tablespoons **apricot jam**

1. Preheat the oven to 160°C fan oven/180°C/Gas 4.

2. Put the apple and water in a small saucepan, bring to the boil, then simmer for 1 minute. Add the sugar and leave to cool.

3. Mix the dry ingredients and the apricots in a bowl.

4. Mix the egg, oil and cooled apple together in a bowl, or jug. Mix into the dry ingredients until everything is evenly distributed.

5. Pour into a greased baking tray and press flat. Bake in the oven for 30 minutes until golden brown on the top.

6. When the cake comes out of the oven, allow to cool for 2–3 minutes. While the cake cools, heat up the jam in a pan until it becomes liquid. Spread the jam over the top of the cake, either with a brush or spoon. Once cool, cut into bars.

Date and Fig Squares

This is a great way to eat dates and figs. These squares have a sticky middle and a contrasting, crumbly, outside.

£ 0.19 /EACH

3

18

PREP 15 MINS

COOK 20 MINS

1/2 x 375g pack of ready-to-eat **stoned dates**, chopped

1/2 x 375g pack of ready-to-eat **figs**, chopped

3/4 mug **water**

grated rind of a **lemon**

1 mug **self-raising flour**

150g **butter** (measure using packet)

1 mug **oats**

1/2 mug brown **sugar**

1. Preheat the oven to 180°C fan oven/200°C/Gas 6.

2. Put the dates, figs, water and lemon rind in a saucepan. Heat gently (but do not boil), until the fruits soften a little.

3. Put the flour into a bowl. Chop the butter up into small pieces and rub into the flour. Add the oats and the sugar and mix. This is the crumble mixture.

4. Put half the crumble mixture in the bottom of a greased baking tray. Spread the fruit mixture evenly over the top. Sprinkle the rest of the dry ingredients over the top and press down gently.

5. Bake in the oven for 20 minutes. The top should be lightly browned. Cut into squares when cool.

Chocolate Truffles

These make good gifts if you wrap them prettily. Keep them in the fridge.

200g block of **dark chocolate**

50g **butter** (measure using packet)

1/3 mug **icing sugar**

2 teaspoons **vanilla extract**

1 mug **ground almonds**,

grated **chocolate**, drinking chocolate, chocolate bits or **icing sugar** to roll the truffles in.

£0.14 /EACH

3

24

PREP 15 MINS

1. Melt the chocolate and the butter in a bowl over a saucepan of simmering water.

2. Add the icing sugar, vanilla extract and the ground almonds. Mix well and leave to cool slightly.

3. Turn out onto a board and cut into 24 pieces. Roll them into balls and then roll in the grated chocolate, drinking chocolate, chocolate bits or icing sugar. Leave in the fridge until required.

Pecan and Chocolate Squares

Desiccated coconut is usually found in the 'baking section' at the supermarket.

2 mugs **rolled oats**

3 tablespoons **desiccated coconut**

125g **butter** (measure using packet)

1/2 mug **brown sugar**

3 tablespoons **golden syrup**

100g pack **pecan** or other nuts, chopped roughly (or a mixture)

100g packet of **chocolate chips**

£0.19 /EACH

2

18

PREP 15 MINS

COOK 25 MINS

1. Preheat the oven to 160°C fan oven/180°C/Gas 4.

2. Put the oats and coconut in a bowl.

3. Put the butter, sugar and syrup in a pan. Heat gently until the sugar has melted. Stir into the oat mixture. Mix well.

4. Press into a greased baking tray. Press the nuts and the chocolate into the top.

5. Cook in the oven for 20-25 minutes until golden brown. Allow to cool in the tray and then cut into pieces.

Chocolate Krispy Munchies

You can ring the changes with this recipe, try cornflakes instead of the Rice Krispies. Also try other chocolate bars, or Maltesers, instead of the Twix bars. These make great gifts, but they do need to be kept in the fridge.

250g bar of milk **chocolate**

1 tablespoon **golden syrup**

1 mug **double cream**

1/2 mug **sugar**

3 mugs **Rice Krispies**

5 x 58g **Twix bars**

1. Line an 18cm x 27cm baking tray with greaseproof paper.

2. Put the chocolate, syrup, cream and sugar into a bowl and place over a pan of simmering water. Melt gently, stirring occasionally. Leave to cool a little.

3. Cut the Twix bars into chunks and place in a large bowl with the Rice Krispies.

4. Quickly stir in the cooled chocolate mixture. Pour into the prepared tray and press down.

5. Leave in the fridge for a couple of hours and then cut into squares.

desserts

Think that making desserts is too difficult, but you have some friends around? Try some of these. Just don't think about the calories!

desserts

Tiramisu

This version is a bit of a cheat, but still tastes fantastic and is really easy.

2 tablespoons **instant coffee**
+ 3 tablespoons **water**

2–3 tablespoons **brandy** or **rum**

1/2 x 175g pack **sponge fingers**

2 x 250g pots of **mascarpone**
cheese

425g tin **custard**

2 tablespoons **icing sugar**

cocoa powder to finish

£0.83 /PERSON

3

4-6

PREP 20 MINS

COOL 1 HOUR

1. Mix the coffee with the water and alcohol. Dip the sponge fingers in the liquid and use them to line the bottom of a bowl. If you do not have a glass bowl, a casserole dish will do.

2. Soften the mascarpone cheese with a spoon and mix in the custard and sugar until it is smooth. Pile on top of the sponge fingers.

3. Leave to set for about 1 hour and then sprinkle cocoa on the top (see photo).

Baked Apples

Easy way to make a dessert for one person. Serve with a little cream, yogurt, crème fraîche, or custard.

£0.58 /PERSON

1

1

PREP 10 MINS

COOK 30 MINS

1 large **cooking apple**

1 tablespoon **brown sugar**

2 tablespoons **sultanas** or **raisins**

a little **butter**

1 dessertspoon **honey**

1. Preheat the oven to 180°C fan oven/200°C/Gas 6.

2. Wash the apple and cut out the core from the centre, leaving the apple whole. Score a horizontal line around the centre of the apple (see photo). This stops the skin from bursting.

3. Mix together the sugar and the fruit. Stuff it into the space where the core was. Place on an ovenproof dish, a casserole dish is fine. Place small pieces of butter around the top of the apple. Spoon the honey over the apple. If you have spare fruit and sugar, sprinkle around the bottom of the apple and it will turn into toffee as the apple cooks.

4. Bake in the oven for 25-30 minutes.

Apple Crumble

You can add many fruits, e.g. blackberries, rhubarb, plums. Cook the fruit in the same way as the apples, taking care not to overcook them and turn them into pulp.

£0.30 /PERSON

2

4

PREP 15 MINS

COOK 25 MINS

2 large **cooking apples**
1/2 mug **water**
1/2 mug **brown sugar** (white is OK)
1/2 teaspoon **mixed spice** (optional)

Topping
1 mug **plain flour**
100g **butter** (measure using packet)
1/2 mug **sugar**

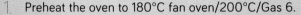

1. Preheat the oven to 180°C fan oven/200°C/Gas 6.

2. Peel the apples and remove the core. Cut into chunks and place in a pan with 1/2 mug of water. Bring to the boil and allow to cook for 3–4 minutes. The apples will begin to go fluffy round the edges and soften. When they do, add the sugar and the mixed spice (if you add the sugar at the beginning, the apples will stay hard). Stir in the sugar and pour into the bottom of an ovenproof dish. A casserole dish will do. Set the dish aside, while you make the topping.

3. Put the flour and butter in a bowl. With your fingers and thumbs, rub the butter into the flour until it looks a bit like breadcrumbs. Add the sugar and mix. Gently spoon on top of the apple mixture and spread evenly. Press down with a fork.

4. Cook in the oven for 20-25 minutes. Serve warm with custard, ice cream, or cream.

Baked Pears with Cinnamon

You can serve this with double cream, crème fraîche, fromage frais, yogurt, ice cream, or custard, depending on the occasion!

2 ripe **pears**

1 tablespoon **lemon juice**

2 tablespoons **brown sugar**

$1/2$ teaspoon ground **cinnamon**

2cm cube **butter**

1 tablespoon **water**

lemon rind to serve (optional)

Serving suggestions

2 tablespoons **yogurt**, **double cream**, **fromage frais**, **crème fraîche**, or **ice cream**

£0.59 /PERSON

2

2

PREP 10 MINS

COOK 25 MINS

1. Preheat the oven to 180°C fan oven/200°C/Gas 6.

2. Peel the pears, halve them and take out the cores. Try to leave the pear halves intact. Place them on the bottom of a greased casserole dish. Brush with the lemon juice as this stops the pears from going brown.

3. Place the sugar, cinnamon, butter and water in a saucepan and bring to the boil. Turn down to a low heat and cook until the sugar is dissolved. Pour over the pears in the casserole dish.

4. Bake for 20-25 minutes. Serve with any of the suggestions above.

Bread and Butter Pud

This is a good way to use up any leftover bread. You can use any type of bread and can add things like chopped up apricots, spoonfuls of marmalade, honey and dried fruits.

3 slices of **bread**

butter to spread

2 tablespoons **sugar**

2 tablespoons **raisins**

3 **eggs**

1 mug **milk**

1/4 teaspoon **cinnamon** (optional)

£0.31 /PERSON

1

2-3

PREP 10 MINS

COOK 25 MINS

1. Preheat the oven to 180°C fan oven/200°C/Gas 6.
2. Spread the bread with butter and cut into 4 triangular pieces. Arrange them in a casserole dish.
3. Sprinkle the sugar and the raisins around the bread.
4. Beat the eggs and add the milk and cinnamon. Pour over the bread.
5. Cook in the oven for 20-25 minutes. The bread should be browned and the eggs set.

Fruity Rice

You can make this with most fruits. Here, I have used fruits of the forest, since they are amongst the most convenient fruits. You can used tinned fruits, but frozen are more healthy, because tinned fruits usually have a lot of sugar added. Fresh fruit is, of course, the best. Strawberries, blackberries, blackcurrants, blueberries and raspberries will work very well.

£0.78 /PERSON

1

2

PREP 5 MINS

425g tin **rice pudding**

½ x 500g pack of frozen **fruits of the forest**, defrosted

1 teaspoon **vanilla extract**

1. Place the rice pudding in a bowl and stir in the vanilla extract.

2. Once the fruit is defrosted, place about 1 tablespoon in the bottom of each dish. If you have glass dishes, that's great, otherwise use cereal bowls. Put half the rice in each bowl. Add more fruit on the top. Serve. Dead easy!

Fruit Fool

You can use other fruits to vary this very easy recipe. Suggested fruits: fruits of the forest, raspberries, mangoes, peaches, blueberries and blackberries. It works best with fresh fruit.

£ 0.61 /PERSON

1

2

PREP 15 MINS

4 sponge fingers

2 tablespoons **orange juice**, or the juice of an orange. You can vary this according to the fruits you use.

2 **kiwi** fruits

6 large **strawberries**

425g pot of fresh **custard**

1/2 x 450g pot of **Greek yogurt** with honey, or any other flavoured yogurt

1. Break the sponge fingers in two. Divide them between 2 bowls. You could use big wine glasses. Pour the orange juice over the sponges.

2. Peel the kiwi fruits and slice thinly. Wash and slice the strawberries.

3. Arrange the fruits, custard and yogurt in 'areas', not so much layers (see photo). Make it look as pretty as possible.

desserts **197**

Sweet Pancakes

Pancakes are good fun when you have friends around. Just make sure others are helping in the cooking process. Tossing them is always fun, but catching them is not guaranteed!

£0.07 /PANCAKE

2

6

PREP 25 MINS

Pancakes

2 **eggs**

6 tablespoons **self-raising flour**

milk (see below)

Trex or white **Flora** to fry (you can use oil but a lard type is best)

Serving suggestions

lemon juice and **sugar**, **undiluted squashes**

any kind of **ice cream**

maple syrup, **golden syrup**

fruit, such as **strawberries**, or **fruits of the forest**

chocolate sauce

1. Beat the eggs and flour together in a bowl or jug. Gradually add enough milk until the mixture is as thin as single cream, i.e. quite thin, but not as thin as milk. Make sure there are no lumps.

2. Heat about 2cm cube of lard in a frying pan. When the fat begins to smoke a little, pour approximately 2 tablespoons of the mixture into the pan. Tip the pan around, so that the mixture spreads over the surface of the pan. Let the mixture cook for about 1 minute.

3. Gently lift the edge of the pancake to see if it is browned. Once browned, turn the pancake with a slotted turner, or toss and then cook the other side. For serving suggestions see above.

Berry Trifle

Very easy to make. Be careful not to beat the cream too much, or you will have made yourself some butter!

1 **chocolate Swiss roll**

500g pack of **frozen summer fruits** or **raspberries**, defrosted

2 tablespoons **icing sugar**

1/2 mug **sherry** or other alcohol

(optional)

425g can of **custard**

1 mug or 1/2 pint of **double cream**

grated **chocolate** or a broken-up **flake** for the topping

£0.67 /PERSON

2

4-6

PREP 20 MINS

COOL 60 MINS

1. Cut about 6–8 slices of the Swiss roll and arrange them on the bottom of a dish. A casserole dish will be fine.

2. Mix the icing sugar with the fruit and distribute evenly over the swiss roll. Allow the juices to seep into the Swiss roll.

3. Pour over the sherry.

4. Pour the custard over the fruit.

5. Beat the cream until it is thick. Carefully spread over the top.

6. Sprinkle the chocolate over the top and leave in the fridge to cool for 1 hour.

Menu 1

Monday Beanburgers p63

Tuesday other beanburger

Wednesday Tomato and Lentil Soup p56

Thursday Quorn Curry p67

Friday rest of Quorn Curry

Saturday ½ quantity Risotto p78

Sunday Leek and Potato Frittata p73

check cupboards for:
- butter
- pickles (for burger)
- red lentils
- Marmite
- Madras curry paste
- raisins
- stock cubes
- oil
- rice
- garlic
- basil
- sugar
- tomato purée
- white wine vinegar

> Here you cook 5 times in the week and share 1 meal. The approximate cost would be £18-20.

Shopping List
- bread
- milk
- cereal
- sandwich fillers
- garlic
- 6 onions
- 1 carrot
- 1 large potato
- 3 small leeks
- 1 sweet potato
- 2 mushrooms
- 1 courgette
- salad (for Sunday)
- 12 eggs (leaves 5 spare for sandwiches)
- 200g pack feta cheese
- 200g pack Cheddar cheese
- 100g pack pine nuts
- 3 x 400g tins chopped tomatoes
- 350g packet frozen chicken style Quorn
- 750g pack frozen broad beans
- 1 bag plain crisps
- 2 bread buns
- Arborio risotto rice

Shopping List

- 2 carrots
- 3 potatoes
- 2 sweet potatoes
- 5 spring onions
- 3 courgettes
- 4 cherry tomatoes
- 3 onions
- 5 mushrooms
- 1 baby aubergine
- 1 red pepper
- 400g tin black-eyed beans
- 250g pack of Cheddar cheese
- 2 x 400g tins chopped tomatoes
- 130g tin sweetcorn
- 6 eggs (5 spare for sandwiches)
- 1 tin cannellini beans
- milk
- bread
- cereal
- sandwich fillers
- couscous
- self-raising flour

Menu 2

Monday Roast Sweet Potatoes with Couscous p74

Tuesday Rest of Sweet Potato

Wednesday Veggie Bake p100

Thursday Rest of Veggie Bake

Friday Shepherd's Pie p160

Saturday rest of Shepherd's Pie

Sunday Corn cakes and Ratatouille - share p98

check cupboards for:

- oil
- tomato purée
- balsamic vinegar
- dried chives
- garlic
- Tobasco or HP sauce
- veg stock
- dried basil
- dried rosemary
- sugar
- butter

This week you cook 4 times and share one. It should cost approximately £20. The shopping list assumes cereal for breakfast and sandwiches for lunch each day.

Menu 3

Monday	Baked Veggie Patties p66
Tuesday	eat rest Baked Veggie Patties
Wednesday	Spag Bol p108
Thursday	eat rest of Spag Bol
Friday	Thai Coconut Veggies p53
Saturday	eat rest of Thai Coconut veggies
Sunday	Tofu Balls p125 - share

check cupboards for:

- veg stock
- oil
- chilli flakes
- oregano
- red lentils
- spaghetti
- garlic
- dried chives
- dried basil
- soy sauce
- flour
- tomato purée
- rice
- Thai red curry paste

Shopping List

- 1 sweet potato
- 2 potatoes
- 5 onions
- 3 carrots
- 1 courgette
- celery
- red pepper
- 250g green beans
- 1 small broccoli
- 6 eggs (leaves 5 spare for sandwiches)
- small carton of double cream
- small piece Parmesan-style cheese
- 2 x 400g tins chopped tomatoes
- 400g can of coconut milk
- 200g pack of Cheddar cheese (plenty spare for sandwiches)
- 375g pack tofu
- bread
- milk
- cereal
- sandwich fillings

Here you cook 4 times and share one meal. Assuming that you eat cereal for breakfast and sandwiches for lunch, should cost approximately £18.

Shopping List

- 4 onions
- 2 tomatoes
- 200g pack fresh spinach
- 1 courgette
- 1 carrot
- salad for Saturday
- 6 eggs
- bread
- milk
- cereal
- sandwich fillings
- 400g tin chickpeas
- 400g tin tomatoes
- frozen peas
- 150g pack Cheddar cheese
- small carton of Greek yogurt
- 100g pack pine nuts
- 200g pack chopped mixed nuts
- natural yogurt

Menu 4

Monday French Onion Soup p55

Tuesday Rest of French Onion Soup

Wednesday Egg Curry p64

Thursday Korma Rice p76

Friday rest of Korma Rice

Saturday Nut and Courgette Slice p116

Sunday rest of Nut and Courgette Slice

check cupboards for:

- oil
- Marmite
- curry paste
- rice
- mango chutney
- garlic
- raisins
- stock cubes

Here you cook 4 times and share once. It should cost you £18-20 assuming cereal for breakfast and sandwiches at lunch.

index

thanks...

This book would not have been possible without the help of many people. My husband Ron and my sons, Ben and Tim, have worked tirelessly to help me.

Thanks again to my very good friends, Fran, for her wonderful proof-reading and to Cathryn, for her help in the kitchen.

Many others came to collect and eat food on our photography days. Without them, much food would have been wasted, which is never a good thing!

Thanks to Tim and Ben's friends who have allowed us to use their faces for the front cover. Your free copy is on it's way!

Josh Smith, Katy Bosanko, Josh Feben, Daniella Clements, Deb Smith, Andy Tiffen, Tommy Andrewartha, Phil Hatton, Felix Page, Jo Skinner, Joel Bennett, Michael Pearce, Rav Hayer, Patrick Wilson, Kat Thomas, Jan Moys, Calum Maciver, Rachel Tiffen, Marianne Matthews, Emma Page, Michelle Crispin, Gareth Matthews, Payin Swazey Attafuah, Mary-Jane Attafuah, Chester See, Ems Smith, Jon Herring, Charlie Gregson, Nathanael Bennett, Paul Cannon, James Malbon, Jess Whitbread, Tom Whitbread, Tim Crispin, Naomi Badu, Rach Clements, Hannah Clements, Naomi Clements, Nathaniel Ledwidge, Tekiva Ledwidge, Peter Kent, Beccy Catley, Matt Bentley, Nicola Goodwin, Leanne Clack, Trudy Willoughby, Cerys Duffty, Amy Banham-Hall, Jonathan Ingham, Tom Povey, Nicole May, Emily Malbon, Ross Macfarlane, Amy Macfarlane, Kirsty Macfarlane, Richard Wells, Juliet Adekambi, Simon William Burns, Sharon Makinde, Rachel Donley, Hannah Rich, Nathan Clements, Rachel Phillipps, Odele Caldecourt, Ben McCalla, Dan Richter, Jon Povey, Peter Goult, Connie Haywood, Jez Hill, Ed Gent, Jenny Copperwheat, Dan Copperwheat, Clarence Bissessar, Sarju Patel, Chris Low, Gabbie D'Mello, Esther Gore, Polly West, Kerry Cannon, Kirsty Crooks, Gareth Paton, Lizzie De Kraan, Jonathan Cannon, Matt Skinner, Luke Clements, Lizzie Fieldsend, Leland Fieldsend and Paul Summerville

Acknowledgements to Daniel Midgley (goodreasonblog.blogspot.com) for the free font we have used in the menus. Love it.

© 2016 Joy May

All rights reserved. No part of this book may be reproduced, stored in a retrieval system, or transmitted, in any form or by any means, electronic, mechanical, photocopying, recording or otherwise without the prior permission of the author.

Published by: Intrade (GB) Ltd

Contact: joymay@mac.com

Author: Joy May

Printed in China

1st Edition: 2006
2nd Edition: March 2011
Revised 2nd Edition: June 2013
Revised 2nd Edition, 4th Print: July 2016

ISBN: 978-0-9543179-7-3

Photography and design: Tim May at www.milkbottlephotography.co.uk

Design: Ben May at www.milkbottledesigns.co.uk

Proof-reading: Fran Maciver

Editor: Ron May